AF600423

ASIAN LAW SERIES
School of Law
University of Washington
Number 9

ASIAN LAW SERIES

School of Law

University of Washington

The Asian Law Series was initiated in 1969, with the cooperation of the University of Washington Press and the Institute for Comparative and Foreign Area Studies (now the Henry M. Jackson School of International Studies), in order to publish the results of several projects under way in Japanese, Chinese, and Korean law. The members of the editorial committee are Herbert J. Ellison, John O. Haley, and Dan Fenno Henderson (chairman).

1. *The Constitution of Japan: Its First Twenty Years, 1947–67*, edited by Dan Fenno Henderson
2. *Village "Contracts" in Tokugawa Japan*, by Dan Fenno Henderson
3. *Chinese Family Law and Social Change in Historic and Comparative Perspective*, edited by David C. Buxbaum
4. *Law and Politics in China's Foreign Trade*, edited by Victor H. Li
5. *Patent and Know-how Licensing in Japan and the United States*, edited by Teruo Doi and Warren L. Shattuck
6. *The Constitutional Case Law of Japan: Selected Supreme Court Decisions, 1961–70*, by Hiroshi Itoh and Lawrence Ward Beer
7. *Japan's Commission on the Constitution: The Final Report*, translated and edited by John M. Maki
8. *Securities Regulations in Korea: Problems and Recommendations for Feasible Reforms*, by Young Moo Shin
9. *Order and Discipline in China: The Shanghai Mixed Court 1911–27*, by Thomas B. Stephens
10. *The Economic Contract Law of China: Legitimation and Contract Autonomy in the PRC*, by Pitman B. Potter

Order and Discipline in China

The Shanghai Mixed Court 1911–27

Thomas B. Stephens

Foreword by Dan Fenno Henderson

University of Washington Press

Seattle and London

Printed in the United States of America

Library of Congress Cataloging-in-Publication Data
Stephens, Thomas B.
Order and discipline in China : the Shanghai Mixed Court 1911–27 / Thomas B. Stephens ; Foreword by Dan Fenno Henderson.
p. cm.
Includes bibliographical references and index.
ISBN 0–295–97123–1 (Asian law series ; no. 9)
1. International Mixed Court (Shanghai, China : International Settlement)—History—20th century. 2. Public policy (Law)—China—Shanghai (International Settlement)—History—20th century. 3. Dispute resolution (Law)—China—Shanghai (International Settlement)—History—20th century. 4. Justice, Administration of—China—Shanghai (International Settlement)—History—20th century. I. Title.
KNQ9035.2.I58S74 1992 91–36748
347.51′13209—dc20 CIP
[345.1132079]

The paper used in this publication meets the minimum requirements of American National Standard for Information Sciences—Permanence of Paper for Printed Library Materials, ANSI Z39.48–1984. ♾

Title page calligraphy by Dr. C. C. S. Young

Contents

Foreword

The Shanghai Mixed Court (1911–27) makes an absorbing story from any angle, but especially from the sharp focus which Dr. Stephens's perspective brings to the story. Combining Chinese and foreigners on the same bench, the court was a unique body started in 1864 and controlled by foreigners after the collapse of the Qing dynasty (1911). Its powers extended to cases by foreigners against Chinese and cases between Chinese. Stephens tells us that the Mixed Court handled a heavy case load reasonably well, despite the wholly different views he finds were held by the Chinese magistrate and foreign assessors on the court as to what they were doing. The differing views, according to Stephens, stem from the fundamental incompatibility between Chinese and Western systems for the maintenance of order in society and for dispute resolution.

As Stephens sees it, the West depends largely on a legal system for these functions, whereas China has no such things, in our sense, as law, courts, or adjudication in its culture; instead it depends solely on a "system of discipline." It is this incisive and provocative analysis of the contrasting perspectives of the Chinese and foreigners as to the mission of the Mixed Court and the role of law in its decisions that will make this study interesting to all students of China. Whether his solution is wholly persuasive or not, Stephens will, I think, sharpen foreign lawyers' understanding of governance in China, past or present. Indeed, as he points out in passing, the ambiguity of current usage of "law" in modern administrative processes immune from judicial review is still suggestive in the modern era of the turgidity of much western writing in English legal terms about Chinese law.

The fundamental point raised is the most basic sort of comparability: Is there an idea or institution comparable to western law, in the deepest and broadest sense, in Chinese philosophy or Chinese governance, past or present? Though it may seem to some to be rather late in the day for such an inquiry, Stephens raises this question forthrightly and answers it clearly: There is no such idea of law in China. Chinese thinking and governance have been based on Confucianistic, elitist authority, on hierarchy and inequality, and on orders, obedience, and duties. In disputes, all is adjustment among the parties or, if needed, instruction from the magistrate, not application of legal rules or assertion of right, as in western adjudication; whereas westerners, from biblical times and the time of ancient Greece onward, have seen "law" as based on principle (universal, given, and external to those bound), and on equality and right, assertable in the adjudicative process from the bottom up by the citizenry.

If there is no adjudication in China, nor any understanding of the idea of law in Chinese culture, and if there is therefore no "right" in China, past or present, surely Stephens is correct in asserting that the analysis and description in much western literature on the Chinese system, proceeding, as it does, in the rhetoric of modern western law, can do little but thoroughly confuse. This is because it wrongly presumes, in a Platonic way, for China the existence of something comparable to our ideas, concepts, and institutions of law. Stephens calls this obfuscating approach "translating backward" all of our legalisms as if they were to be found in the Chinese system.

With confident clarity, Stephens tells us that this was exactly the case in the past: from the time of the early missionaries onward, most western scholars of Chinese "law" have failed to study, understand, or describe the system as it is, that is, as a simple disciplinary system, lacking law, courts, or adjudication. Rather, several generations of foreign scholars of Chinese "law" have tended, uncritically, to "translate backward" into the Chinese milieu our own legalisms, and therefore they, and of course their readers, inevitably find "law" where it has never been. This is a strong position, seldom if ever so emphatically argued, despite several prestigious harbingers of Stephens's position, as he points out.

There is a certain elegance as well as persuasiveness to the argument, which inheres in Stephens's artful selection of the Mixed Court in Shanghai as a case-study to demonstrate concretely in daily operation the basic differences between the two systems (law and discipline). We are shown the lack of comparability between the essentials of our legal system and the Chinese disciplinary system by observing the travail of this unique court in its Chinese setting comprised of foreign judges and Chinese administrators (not judges). They worked together to resolve disputes from entirely different views of the basic tenets of governance.

At a superficial level, one can see that this is at least in part a language problem. Stephens is saying that we are getting too much use out of "law," "court," "judge," and other legal terms, by using the same word to denote two or more things. Opponents might feel that he is trying to appropriate to his own cause exclusive use of these good words. But, though part of the problem Stephens is attacking is one of definition, as with the sloppy usage found in abundance in modern jurisprudence, there is surely more to it. There is lawyer's law—rules applied by independent courts; and there are the orders—do-as-you-are-told-and-don't-talk-back "law"—of disciplinary systems. Indeed there is plenty of de facto do-as-you-are-told "law" in modern administration, side by side with real justiciable law, and we continually call them both, in all sorts of contexts, simply "law." Even if he did nothing else, Stephens makes a good case for two names for these two kinds of everyday "law": justiciable law and from-top-down, unchallengeable administrative orders.

But Stephens's significance is not confined to this kind of quibbling. His point is that there is no way to understand and describe the sophisticated workings of Chinese governance, past or present, without starting from premises in the philosophy, the culture, and the sociology of China; and these know no formal adjudication as we know it today. The Chinese system is different indeed. Therefore, the Chinese system must have its own language. As Stephens would say, it needs the language of a "disciplinary system." Terminology from a "legal system" will only confuse by causing readers to think we are discussing comparative law.

Stephens's point goes much deeper. There is no place for comparative law in understanding China, because there is no law of our sort there, no justiciable rules, independent bar, independent bench, or adjudication, and we should save our legal terms for our system, so as to distinguish our penchant for justiciable law from techniques the Chinese use to maintain order and to settle disputes. This will not only clarify our thinking, but enable us to understand and appreciate better Chinese thinking, unencumbered by law.

Stephens's analysis comes at a good time as we continue to study and increasingly, it seems, to embrace so-called alternative dispute resolution in this country. In China these techniques have always been the mainstream, not alternatives at all. Presumably our embracing of these, for us, newly found methods is in part a recognition of the limitations of our legal system in serving all of our people. This recognition in turn would logically imply some appreciation for the Chinese ways, and force us to reevaluate both systems which Stephens analyzes for us. His point deserves careful attention.

Seattle, 1991 DAN FENNO HENDERSON

Preface

The ensuing pages offer a short history of the Mixed Court of the International Settlement at Shanghai from 1911 to 1927 and an assessment of its work over those years. The International Settlement was a large enclave of foreigners of many nationalities established on the river Huangpu near Shanghai for purposes of trade. By treaty, all but a few of the foreigners enjoyed the benefits of extraterritoriality—they were exempt from the application of Chinese law and were not subject to any Chinese authority. Within the settlement boundaries the foreigners were supreme, taxing, policing, and governing themselves and the numerous Chinese living there. It was a self-contained community politically independent of China and Chinese control. The foreigners set up a municipal council to regulate the domestic affairs of the settlement and established their own national courts for dispute resolution and the maintenance of order among themselves. In 1925 the settlement occupied 8.7 square miles of Chinese territory, and its population numbered 30,000 foreigners and 810,000 Chinese. It had developed into the biggest and most important commercial and banking center in all China.

The Mixed Court of the International Settlement dealt with people of Chinese nationality accused of offenses or crimes committed within settlement limits and was responsible for dispute resolution, criminal administration, and the enforcement of order generally for the very large Chinese component of the population. Since the foreigners had no jurisdiction over Chinese nationals on Chinese soil, they arranged for a Chinese magistrate to sit for this purpose within settlement limits. But they insisted that a western consular representative (called an assessor) should sit with him to monitor the proceedings and to ensure that western interests were protected and the proceedings were conducted as far as possible according to western ideals of criminal administration and judicial independence and probity. The Chinese magistrate and the western assessor sitting together made up the Mixed Court.

Heretofore the Mixed Court has conventionally been looked upon as a court of law administering a legal system, and its results have been evaluated against a background of jurisprudence or the theory of law. Chinese jural processes, however, do not respond convincingly to treatment in such terms, and accordingly the perspective in which the subject is developed here is a new one. In this work the Mixed Court is interpreted and evaluated not as a court of law but as a disciplinary tribunal enforcing a system of dispute resolution and the maintenance of social order upon the principles of disciplinary theory rather than of jurisprudence or legal theory. For convenience and for the better understanding of the Chinese system, I have included in chapter 2 a short formulation of some of the major principles of disciplinary theory.

The Mixed Court provides a particularly advantageous observation point to measure the two systems—the legal and the disciplinary—against each other and to study them in conflict, since it was a point of direct confrontation between them, a point where they met in head-on collision and resisted all attempts at reconciliation.

The importance of the study of disciplinary theory is that it provides an alternative framework of principles in terms of which a much more credible and convincing picture of Chinese processes of dispute resolution and the enforcement of order can be projected than any that is possible in terms of the principles, concepts, and vocabulary of familiar Western legal systems. Indeed it may be affirmed that only a grossly distorted caricature and a grave misrepresentation of the Chinese system is possible without the insights that a study of disciplinary theory affords.

This book represents a closely condensed version of my doctoral dissertation. I have relied for my sources largely upon the British Foreign Office files in the Public Record Office in London, the United States Department of State Archives in Washington, and the files of the *North China Herald, Supreme Court Reporter and Consular Gazette*, a British newspaper published in Shanghai. The original records of the Mixed Court itself are not available. In 1957 Jean Chesneaux reported that he had been allowed access to the archives of the secretariat of the Municipal Council of the International Settlement at Shanghai, which is where one would expect to find the Mixed Court records if they still exist, but he searched for them in vain. Probably they have not survived the Japanese occupation and the Communist takeover.

In 1979 Nicholas R. Clifford reported that all his attempts to gain permission to see the municipal council archives proved fruitless. My own attempt to raise the matter with Chinese authorities was sternly rebuffed.

I can however report that in the Public Record Office in London, research disclosed an unexpected but very welcome source of original material of great interest that I have never seen previously referred to: the correspondence files of the British assessors on the Mixed Court from 1906 to 1927. These files are incomplete and vary very much in size and quality from year to year, but they often include actual examples of Mixed Court process and copies of judgments and documents from the missing Mixed Court files, as well as a wealth of ancillary and highly illuminating material.

These files afford an invaluable insight into the workings of the Mixed Court, and I have drawn upon them heavily in my account. They are scattered among the much more numerous and much bulkier correspondence files of a totally unrelated court—"His Britannic Majesty's Supreme Court for China and Corea"—and are to be found under the class number for that court, FO 656, but are now separately noted in the indexes.

I have relied also for source material upon interviews and correspondence with a number of survivors of the Mixed Court period in Shanghai whom I have been able to contact, and I owe my thanks to all of these for their contributions. Among them I am particularly grateful to Dr. John C. H. Wu, Dr. C. H. Kao, Mr. N. F. Allman, and the late Sir John Keswick for their willing cooperation and the special illumination they were able to throw upon the subject of my study. Dr. Wu and Dr. Kao were judges on the bench of the Jiangsu Provisional Court which took over the work of the Mixed Court when that court was abolished in 1927. Mr. N. F. Allman was the American assessor on the bench of the Mixed Court from 1922 to 1924 and thereafter practiced law in the International Settlement until 1941. Sir John Keswick was chairman of directors of Jardine Matheson & Co. Ltd.

I am deeply indebted to many distinguished sinologists, lawyers, and scholars both in Australia and overseas for the encouragement, guidance, and assistance they have given me in my work over the years. Especially I should mention with gratitude for their interest and inspiration Professor J. Duncan M. Derrett and Dr. Mark Elvin in England, Professor Karl Bünger in Germany, and Professor Dan F. Henderson, Professor Jerome Cohen, and Professor William C. Jones in the United States.

It is a pleasure to acknowledge the unfailing courtesy and ready help offered at all times by the staff and the assistants at the Public Record Office, London, and by the librarians and staff at the School of Oriental and African Studies and the Institute of Advanced Legal Studies in London, at the Australian National University, and at the National Library of Australia in Canberra. My thanks are also due to the Institute of Modern History at the Academia Sinica in Taipei for allowing me access to the archives of the Foreign Affairs Ministry R.O.C. in the custody of the institute.

I should add that none of the statements, views, arguments, opinions or attitudes expressed or implied in this work are to be attributed to any of the persons whose help I have acknowledged but are to be laid, together with the errors and shortcomings of the work, solely at my door.

Brisbane, 1991 T. B. STEPHENS

Note on Romanization

The English-language sources for the period with which this work is concerned, particularly the *North China Herald* law reports, offer Chinese names in a variety of strange forms often corresponding to no known system of Romanization. Chinese characters for the names are seldom given. In such cases accurate transliteration into Pinyin is not feasible and there is no point in attempting it.

Jean Chesneaux and John Lust in their *Introduction aux études d'histoire contemporaine de Chine 1898–1949* declare, "In the case of an obscure litigant in a Mixed Court case reported in the *North China Herald*, generally one cannot hope to recover the Chinese characters for his name and accordingly it is not possible to convert the name into any accepted system." In cases where this difficulty arises the name is simply reproduced in this work in the same form as it occurs in the sources.

In the case of a Chinese author who has published in English under a particular name, as Paul Heng-chao Ch'en or T'ung-tsu Ch'ü or John C. H. Wu, one does not presume to alter the name he himself has chosen to be known by. Nor does one alter the titles of published works or quotations from such works.

Otherwise Pinyin is used throughout. Generally when a Pinyin form is first used, the more familiar Wade-Giles or hitherto commonly accepted form will follow in parentheses, thus: Beijing (Peking).

CHAPTER 1

Order without Law

When traditional Chinese concepts and ideals of social order, interpersonal relations and obligations, and dispute resolution are viewed against the familiar models of Western jurisprudence, it is found that the two by no means coincide. This nonconformity has long embarrassed Western jurists attempting to interpret the Chinese system in terms of Western juristic thought and to analyze it in terms of comparative law. The disparities are notorious and profound. It was the nature and extent of these disparities that gave rise to extraterritoriality in China and gave the Western powers reason to continue it as late as 1943.

The fundamental difficulty is that the Chinese system simply does not yield to treatment in terms of Western jurisprudence or legal theory. The realities of dispute resolution and the maintenance of social order in traditional China do not fit, and cannot be made to fit, into the categories, constructs, and relationships of Western jurisprudence. An entirely different framework of theory, unrelated to jurisprudence, is called for if the realities of the Chinese system are to be made intelligible in Western thought patterns.

In this chapter, therefore, an alternative basis of theory upon which to interpret the Chinese system is proposed, namely the theory of disciplinary systems of order. A much more realistic and credible picture of how the Chinese system actually worked and how it differed from the Western can be projected in terms of the principles of disciplinary theory than any which is possible in terms of conventional legal theory.

We are not greatly concerned here with resemblances or differences in the substantive content of the respective norms of preferred conduct to be found in the two systems. In many respects there were close resemblances. Both systems assumed that it is wrong to murder or steal, that fraud should be discouraged and punished, that debts must be paid, guarantees honored, and so on. In other respects substantial differences appeared, particularly in family matters and in criminal administration. But we are not concerned here with such differences as how many wives or concubines a man may take, who succeeds to land when the landholder dies, what conduct is deemed to merit the death penalty, and so on. Such considerations are primarily of sociological, political, and economic significance and only secondarily of jurisprudential interest.

We are concerned here with deeper issues, with fundamental divergencies in the theoretical and philosophical concepts of the nature and purposes of the processes of dispute resolution and the maintenance of order in society. It is at this level that the divergencies occur that give rise to the intractable problems met with in attempting to reconcile the two systems.

Examination and analysis of the differences at this level, made in the classic works of Marcel Granet,[1] Jean Escarra,[2] and Joseph Needham,[3] point to the conclusion that the discrepancies between the two systems rest ultimately, not in differing concepts of law, but at a much deeper level in differing concepts of order.

In Western thought, the antithesis of chaos is order, and order is conceived of, both cosmologically and philosophically, as an artificial objective deliberately brought about, managed, and controlled in predetermined forms according to the conscious will of a transcendent power exterior to the flux, by the enforcement of codes of rigid, universal, specific, imperatives constraining conduct.[4]

In Chinese thought and cultural tradition, the antithesis of chaos is harmony, which is thought of simply as a natural characteristic of a state of affairs that arises and persists automatically in a hierarchical universe so long as all the individual parts of that universe, even the smallest, and all persons in it, perform their duties and offices faithfully "according to the internal necessities of their own natures" in whatever station or function in life they find themselves born to or assigned to by superior authority.[5]

The difference between these two contrasting states of order and of harmony is reflected in the means adopted to sustain them. In Western society, where concepts of order prevail, disputes are resolved and breaches of order are corrected by measuring them against rigid, universal codes of imperatives external to the parties, in an adjudication. This adjudication is conducted by an authority equally subject to the codes, independent of each of the parties, and not committed to the interests of either one more than the other, and regardless of the consequences to the existing social and political order and the policies of its rulers.[6] The outcome turns on the balancing of the rights and duties of each party in relation to the other according to the predetermined codes. This may be designated an "adjudicative" system. Rules of obligation are the heart and center of this system.[7] It is not inappropriate therefore, following H. L. A. Hart and Lon L. Fuller, to refer to this category alternatively as a "legal" system.

In the society of traditional China, where concepts of harmony prevailed, disputes were resolved and disturbances of harmony corrected (ideally within the immediate group where they arose) by relating them to the personalities, the exigencies, and the surrounding circumstances of the particular case, with a view to the instruction of the parties in the conduct expected of them, and the punishment of those disturbing harmony. This process was carried out by, and according to the values of, an authority superior in rank to both parties (generally from among the leaders of the immediate group), and primarily in the interests of maintaining the existing hierarchical order, the superior position of the authority figures in it, and the cohesion of the group.[8] The outcome in such a system turns upon the enforcement of duties without rights. This may be designated a "disciplinary" system.[9] Obedience to superiors in a hierarchy of authority is the heart and center of this system. It does not use the idea of transcendent, rigid, predetermined, universal, and imperative rules. We may adopt the word used by Alice Ehr-Soon Tay in connection with the Chinese system and label this category, alternatively, a "parental" system.[10]

It is characteristic of the adjudicative system that political rulers applying it act as the "fountain of justice," that is to say they concern themselves in their subjects' quarrels and actively enforce their subjects' rights according to the transcendent codes of imperatives and the independent adjudicator's judgments.

It is characteristic of the disciplinary system that the political rulers or supreme hierarchical authorities applying it concern themselves as little as possible with the quarrels of subordinates. It is the very definite duty of the lower ranks and the common people not to quarrel at all, and if they do they must at all costs settle it among themselves, and certainly not on any account trouble their ruler or any government officials with it. If they do, they must expect to be treated harshly—especially the complainant who brought the trouble to the notice of the officials.

Some of the more obvious differences and direct contrasts between the two modes of social control have been exemplified in the table on p. 6.

The practical incidents of adjudicative systems of order are matters of commonplace knowledge and experience in the West. They are the daily concern of every practicing lawyer. The theory and philosophy of adjudicative systems have been for centuries the subject of intensive

The Adjudicative (or "Legal")	*The Disciplinary (or "Parental")*
Contemplates: a confrontation between parties on an equal footing, an external fixed code of conduct not prescribed by either, and enforced by an authority equally subject to it, independent of each of the parties, and not committed to the interests of either one more than the other, regardless of the consequences to the existing political order. The proceedings turn on rights.	*Contemplates:* a confrontation between unequals—a status superior and an inferior—where an alleged insubordination is investigated and punished by one of the parties, i.e., the superior (or a delegate) and primarily in the interests of that party, and of maintaining the existing hierarchical order and the superior's own authority in it. The proceedings turn on duties.
Rules prescribing conduct are: central, indispensable, and of the essence.	*Rules prescribing conduct are:* peripheral, dispensable, and, if used at all, for convenience only.
Observable in: the West, the United States, Europe, and in sports.	*Observable in:* Asia, China, Japan, and in the armed forces.
Appropriate to a society classed as: individualistic and egalitarian, "contract oriented," "*Gesellschaft,*"* or "organized."	*Appropriate to a society classed as:* group hierarchical, "status oriented," "*Gemeinschaft,*"* or "fragmented."
Links that bind society together are: reciprocal ties of mutual rights and obligations enforced horizontally between equals.	*Links that bind society together are:* unilateral ties of duty only, enforced vertically downward upon inferiors.
Behavioral guides: please yourself so long as you do not break the rigid rules. Lawyers, courts, and judges tell you what you must do according to universal fixed codes, e.g., acts of Parliament.	*Behavioral guides:* please your group leaders at whatever cost. Your group leaders will tell you what to do (in traditional China, even what man or woman you must marry), according to what is best for the group in the particular circumstances of each case.
Theory of this category: jurisprudence.	*Theory of this category:* nowhere systematically formulated.

**Gesellschaft* refers to a group of people bound together into an association by artificial and adventitious ties such as laws, the constitution, the rules of a club, or the terms of a business contract. A trading company incorporated under some legislative act is an example. *Gemeinschaft* refers to a group of people bound together into a community by natural and enduring ties, such as ties of blood, race, religion, or tradition. The family is an example. For the signification of these indicators in the classification of societal structures in sociology, see Ferdinand Tonnies, *Community and Society*, trans. and ed. Charles P. Loomis (New York: Harper & Row, 1957), 37–102; Eugene Kamenka, "Gemeinschaft and Gesellschaft," *Political Science* (New Zealand) 17, no. 1 (1965): 3–12.

study and research in the field of jurisprudence. A voluminous body of literature has accumulated.

The practical incidents of disciplinary systems of order are also by no means unfamiliar in the West. Every child is born into a disciplinary system—that of the nursery. The earliest lessons that the child learns of the enforcement of social restraints and standards of behavior in society are taught through the medium of disciplinary systems—those of the family and the schoolroom. In adult life many of the incidents of a modified disciplinary system become well known to those who serve in the armed forces. Relatively strict disciplinary systems for the maintenance of order may be observed in the study of the armies of ancient Rome or of Europe up to about the time of Wellington. Some religious orders in the past have offered instructive examples of the disciplinary mode of social control.[11] In England a vestige of disciplinary authority still remains in the universities, but the exercise of it is no longer autonomous. It stems from statute or from contract and it is subject to review by the judges, according to principles of law.[12]

The theory and philosophy of disciplinary systems however has received almost no attention at all at the hands of scholars, either in China or in the West. No comprehensive or systematic formulation of the principles of such systems has yet been attempted. This deficiency will be returned to later in the chapter.

It should be noticed that the two categories specified here—the adjudicative and the disciplinary—are intended as categories of modes of social control and nothing more. They are not intended to categorize types of political authority, leadership or domination, structures of society, or government, but merely modes of dispute resolution and the maintenance of order. These two modes, or some recognizable characteristics of them, may be found in a variety of different types of society and under a variety of governmental styles. Attention is being directed here only to the type and mode of operation of the order machinery, not to the form and characteristics of the total society, or of the total governmental complex. Furthermore, although other types of order control might well be singled out for attention and categorized, the purposes of this work call for an understanding only of the two types that have been specified and an exploration of the differences between them.

There is nothing new in the suggestion that the traditional Chinese system of dispute resolution and the maintenance of order in society was cast in a disciplinary mold. An analogy with parental control of order in the nursery and family has been consistently recognized since before Confucius.[13] Max Weber reaffirmed the analogy and enunciated it in his account of the Chinese system in terms of a "patriarchal" and fatherly administration and his identification of the dispute settlement aspects of it with "the intrafamilial mode of settling conflicts."[14] Intrafamilial settlement of disputes is, of course, a textbook example of a group disciplinary system in action. Tay, commenting on Weber, points out that "the overwhelming majority of Western observers have felt that traditional Chinese justice is 'parental' rather than 'adjudicative' justice."[15]

Jerome A. Cohen, explaining and illustrating the philosophy underlying the criminal process in China today, has aligned it with the attitudes of the Inquisition and the practices of nursery management, both of which are exemplary disciplinary systems.[16] The consistent use by the Chinese themselves, since very ancient times, of the "father and mother" image of state authority invites, if it does not demand, a disciplinary interpretation of social order in China.

Neither is there anything original or strange in the thought that the traditional Chinese system of order was not a legal system.[17] In 1934, Marcel Granet observed, "La notion Chinoise de l'Ordre exclut, sur tous ses aspects, l'idée de Loi" (The Chinese notion of Order excludes, in all its aspects, the idea of Law).[18] Joseph Needham, after the most extensive and searching investigations, approved Granet's observation, finding that the Chinese see order in the universe, and therefore in society, as a case of "Order which excludes Law."[19] What is present is the harmony of pattern arising spontaneously from within. The idea of predetermined, rigid, universal imperatives governing conduct and imposing order from without is not there.[20] Nor is there any word in the Chinese language which projects that idea, as does the English word "law." The character *fa*, 法, is often translated "law" but the two words are not by any means equivalent. The expression *fa* conveys primarily a signification of "model" or "method." Its connotations are primarily persuasive and exemplary rather than imperative. Even when it is used to convey specifically an imperative signification, that signification does not project the idea of universal, compulsive, rigid rules of general behavior external to the parties, but only the idea of the immediate command of a present superior in a hierarchical social context.[21] Watt sharply distinguishes *fa* from law, rejecting the translation "law" and rendering it as "methods."[22]

In the teaching of the *Fa Jia*, the so-called School of Legalists, the art of government was not seen as resting only, nor even chiefly, in *fa*.[23] The role of *fa* was similar to that of the standing orders of a military or command headquarters, issued from time to time for obedience by all under command as a manifesto expressing the commander's will for the time being and as a means of maintaining instant response to that will at all times. The use of the word *legalism* in this connection is unfortunate and misleading. As Fung Yu-lan has pointed out, "It is wrong to associate the thought of the Legalist School with jurisprudence."[24] The teaching of the legalists was directed to administration, organization, and leadership, not legalism. Waley calls the followers of this way of thought "realists" not "legalists."[25]

Szaszy, investigating the concept of the legal rule in different cultures, found that in China legality as a principle was abhorred, and that, according to Chinese theory,

> the notion of subjective law, of the legal relation, rigidly opposes the idea of natural order. Subjective law, or the legal relation, is a form of social disease. The making of legal rules is the original evil; honesty and morals, and not the law, have to be the guides of human conduct.[26]

George W. Keeton observed in 1928, and his remarks were echoed in 1939 by Marc van der Valk, that no one had, so far, been able to link up the Chinese system with the "main-stream of the world's legal progress" as Sir Henry Maine had done for the Hindu system.[27] No one had been able to relate the Chinese system to the main legal systems of the world according to the methods of comparative jurisprudence.[28] The position is the same today. The Chinese system is still treated by legal comparatists as a nonconforming system, sui generis, and beyond the pale of the world's legal systems. Thus René David and John Brierley in a 560-page book on *Major Legal Systems in the World Today* devote only twelve pages to the consideration of the Chinese system (which has persisted for two thousand years and serves one-quarter of all mankind), and they include in those twelve pages their account not only of the traditional Chinese system but of the modern socialist system as well. They find that the Chinese "normally live outside or apart from the law" and that "in China today, the principle of legality, which has never gained any intellectual hold nor become established in practice, has been repudiated."[29] They do not attempt to explain nor even to name the system of principles by which the Chinese do live and maintain social order in their extra-legal society. So also, the editors of the monumental *International Encyclopedia of Comparative Law*, finding that "the Far East and Black Africa reject the idea of law as a principle,"[30] have afforded the Chinese system, in all their vast undertaking, only eight pages in a very generalized and discursive essay on "The Far Eastern Conception of Law."[31]

Antony Allott declines to be drawn into any discussion of the Chinese system of dispute resolution and the maintenance of social order, traditional or modern, dismissing the subject with an enigmatic "China's *Law* still remains largely a thing unknown."[32]

"It is exceedingly difficult to know how to study Chinese Law. . . . The essential elements of our law had no 'legal' significance whatever in China," writes William C. Jones.[33]

In the light of such considerations as these it can hardly be said that there is anything novel or extraordinary in the thought that however one may treat the Chinese system, it cannot be sound to interpret it in terms of a legal system.

Nevertheless, conventionally and almost universally, Chinese processes of dispute resolution and the maintenance of order have been, and in the main still are, described and discussed in the terminology and against a background of the conceptual framework of the jurisprudence and the legal structures of the modern West.

This approach has its dangers. It can easily betray an author into what Bohannan has called "backward translation,"[34] the process of starting with an English word and then finding a foreign institution to attach it to, instead of starting with the foreign institution and finding English words to describe it. In this way judges, magistrates, law courts, law codes, statutes, legislation, legal proceedings, litigation, trials, lawsuits, contracts, territorial sovereignty, due process, and all the paraphernalia of the legal subcultures of Western constitutional democracies have been exported from the West and smuggled into China. These figures and entities have proliferated so freely in Western writings on China that they have gone far to obscure and to smother the reality of Chinese jural processes. The truth is that the offices of judge and magistrate, the conduct of law courts and legal proceedings, the implications of due process and statute law, and the elements of contract and many other legal relations in Western jurisprudence connote principles, concepts, and procedures that were not within the horizons of thought of any Chinese administrative official from the lowest *zhixian* up to the board of punishments and to the emperor himself.

Thus the *zhixian,* properly a District Imperial Disciplinary Surrogate for Taxation, Public Order, and General Administration, is labeled "district magistrate" and cast, incongruously and uncomfortably, in the role of an adjudicative official, a type of functionary unknown in disciplinary systems.

Thus also John Henry Wigmore, one of America's most illustrious jurists and a distinguished Japanologist, in his *Panorama of the World's Legal Systems* published in 1928, declared, in his section on the Chinese system, that "Confucius . . . was a chief justice about B.C. 500. . . . He spent his life in many provinces as a statesman, a philosopher, and a judge, uniting in one man the careers of a Jefferson, an Emerson and a Marshall."[35]

In fact Confucius would have recoiled in horror from the principles that motivate a chief justice and from the ideals that motivated the careers of President Jefferson, Chief Justice Marshall, and transcendentalist Emerson. He would have regarded them as treasonable and immoral and as tending to the destruction of all civilized society and all order in the universe.

The danger is that the indiscriminate use of familiar Western terminology and the names of familiar Western institutions for the discrepant and only distantly related entities of an Asian culture tends to distort the image and rather to conceal than to reveal the Asian reality by hiding it behind a Western mask.

Nevertheless, most sinologists continue to hang their discussions of Chinese dispute resolution and Chinese processes of social order upon a framework of the concepts and terminology of the jurisprudence and legal institutions of the modern West.[36] Why do they do this? Perhaps the basic reason is simply because there exists no alternative framework of disciplinary theory ready at hand for sinologists to use.

CHINA

Living for more than two thousand years in a relationship with their rulers that they themselves characterized as a parent-child relationship, the Chinese were very experienced in the practical application of a parental or disciplinary system of order. There developed moreover in China a considerable literature on dispute resolution and the maintenance of order in society. Interest, however, was concentrated on the substantive specifications of preferred behavior in particular circumstances, on the proper punishments for misbehavior, and on the realities of particular cases. It was not directed to the theory of the systems as such.

There never developed in China any sustained interest in the investigation and study of the system or process of the maintenance of order considered in the abstract, apart from the substantive content of the norms it upheld.[37] Escarra puts it thus:

There lacked in China that tradition of jurisconsults succeeding one another through the centuries, whose opinions, independent of the positive law and whatever its practical application might be, built up, on account of their methodical, doctrinal, and scientific character, the "theory" or speculative part of law.[38]

Chinese genius was never inspired to erect the analysis of the Chinese system into a formal science of the theory of the maintenance of order that might stand in the same relation to the Chinese system as jurisprudence stands to the legal systems of the West.

THE WEST

In the West the disciplinary mode of social control has never attracted to itself the same degree of scholarly study and interest as that accorded to the legal mode. A proportionate proliferation of literature never occurred. Doubtless this is partly accounted for by the relatively simple nature of the former as against the infinite complexity of the latter. But the point must also be made that in the West since the close of the Middle Ages the importance of discipline as a mode of exercising leadership and authority over large bodies of men has steadily declined. With the coming of the Renaissance in Europe a spectacular rise of interest in law and in legal systems began and has persisted to the present day. In the event, the study of legal theory became raised to the dignity of a science, while the study of disciplinary theory has been almost totally neglected.

MILITARY SOURCES

A surprisingly small literature emanates from military sources on discipline. Army manuals and textbooks take discipline for granted as an unchallengeable datum and discuss it almost solely from the practical point of view—how it should be maintained and exercised to the best advantage for morale and fighting efficiency. Characteristically the approach tends to be that of discipline in action—a parade-ground address—rather than that of discipline in theory—dispassionate analysis.[39]

Army sources disclose no significant interest in the construction of a framework of theory that might serve as a standard in terms of which to discuss and evaluate disciplinary systems generally.

JURISPRUDENCE AND THE COURTS

Jurisprudence and courts of law in the West are concerned with the study and implementation of a legal system in a rule-of-law society. Naturally enough they evince very little interest in the extralegal processes of the disciplinary administration of order.

Until recently the courts in England have generally shown considerable reluctance to concern themselves in any way with the proceedings of disciplinary authorities. As late as 1954 in *Ex parte Fry*[40] the Court of Appeal refused to review the exercise of disciplinary authority over a fireman by the chief officer of the fire brigade. Since the decision in *Ridge v. Baldwin* (1964),[41] however, the courts have insisted that all tribunals, judicial or otherwise, must act *fairly* whenever they are called upon to give a decision affecting the legitimate rights or interests of others and that the courts will correct them if they do not.

In English law there is now no basis for disciplinary rules and procedures unless they are authorized by contract or by statute.[42] The autonomy of disciplinary systems based on status and operating outside the purview of the courts is no longer admitted.

It is hardly surprising therefore that one will not find in jurisprudence or in the decisions of the judges any systematic presentation of the theoretical principles of a disciplinary system of order based on status, self-constituted, and independent of any legal foundation.

LEGAL SOCIOLOGY AND POLITICAL SCIENCE

In the sociology of law and in political science the maintenance of order in some societies is seen as resting upon a direct authority relationship of domination-submission between ruler and ruled exercised at large outside the constraints of any legal system and supported partly by coercion and partly by a greater or lesser degree of consent on the part of those ruled.

There is an infinite variety of forms of this type of control, ranging from the total consent and blind faith of a religious community in the domination of a spiritual leader to the opposite extreme of almost total reliance by a hated tyrant upon force and terror. It is in this range of control techniques that the characteristics of the disciplinary mode may chiefly be found.

Legal sociology and political science however do not provide the further refinement of analysis we are seeking. The essential elements of the disciplinary mode have not been extracted and isolated from the many instances where they occur, and no systematic formulation of the principles of disciplinary systems has been presented.

Max Weber, it is true, has devoted some eight pages to a discussion of discipline.[43] But he uses the word only to mean a technique for enhancing the effectiveness of the efforts of teams of workers in the achievement of a specific objective. He recognizes the decisive role that discipline plays in securing the obedience of subordinates and maintaining effective superiority over them. He does not however offer any theory of discipline considered purely for itself as a principle of order in human society generally, irrespective of the ideals or purposes for which any particular society may be ordered.

It is apparent that there is lacking both in Chinese and in Western scholarship the theoretical framework of principles that the historian needs in order to present for Western comprehension an accurate picture of Chinese processes and institutions of social order. What is required is not merely a "folk system" for the case of China but a general theory adapted for the analysis of all nonlegal types of domination-submission insofar as any of them make use of aspects and features of the disciplinary mode.[44] The relevance of such a general theory would not be limited to sinological studies. It would offer a general alternative frame of reference applicable in many situations where the concepts and principles of law and jurisprudence are clearly inadequate and inappropriate for the interpretation and evaluation of the social and political realities.

It is not possible in this work to offer a comprehensive formulation of a "Science of the Theory and Philosophy of Disciplinary Systems of Dispute Resolution and of the Maintenance of Social Order." In view however of the methodological deficiency occasioned by the absence of any authoritative work on the subject, an attempt will be made in the next chapter to formulate briefly some of the major principles of disciplinary theory, especially those that are relevant to the understanding of the problems of the Mixed Court and the assessment of its achievements. The principles so displayed will serve also to illustrate some of the contrasts and basic incompatibilities between disciplinary theory on the one hand and the familiar tenets of legal theory, or jurisprudence, on the other. They will also indicate some of the kinds of adjustments the Western lawyer seeking to understand disciplinary systems will be required to make.

It should be noticed in passing that the contrasts and incompatibilities which will appear do not define the totality of the divergencies between the Chinese and the Western systems of social order by any means. They are only the tip of an iceberg. In a philosophic examination, F. S. C. Northrop found that the differing cultures of the Far East and the West arise from differing cosmological origins and can only be understood in terms of epistemologically different worlds of discourse, and that such systems are not directly intercommunicable—the one cannot be expressed or comprehended in terms of the other. This arises out of the circumstance that these different epistemologies connote not merely different ways of reasoning, but different ways of perceiving nature, different ways of "knowing."[45] Such philosophic analyses go deeper than we need to go for our present purposes, but they are relevant here to enable us to maintain a proper perspective on the magnitude of the intellectual and cultural gap underlying the obvious differences that appear on the surface in the confrontation of the two systems.

CHAPTER 2

An Introduction to the Study of the Principles of Disciplinary Theory

The principles of the theory and philosophy of disciplinary systems must be sought for in the observation and study of the actual operation of such systems in their objective reality on the ground, wherever they may occur.

It is from the operation and administration of army discipline, of the parental aspects of government, and of dispute resolution in the group-hierarchical societies of China and Japan that the principles hereunder developed have chiefly been ascertained. There is no space here to support their derivation by argument, but I believe there is nothing new or startling in any of them, and that any person reflecting on the maintenance of order in the nursery, the schoolroom, in military forces, and in the traditional societies of China and Japan will be readily able to recognize and accept these principles as underlying to a greater or lesser degree the orderly conduct of those communities.

In relation to military sources, however, some caution is necessary. In any attempt to formulate these principles, it is the autonomous authority deriving purely from status and naturally inherent in superior ranks in a hierarchical society that must be sought for and studied. The authority exercised by commanders in the armies of the West today is no longer one of that kind. It is no longer the self-supporting *imperium* inherent in the concept of military command that it once was, but a mere creature of statute, deriving from, and limited by, some legislative act within the adjudicative administration of a constitutional democracy. Discipline in the armies of the West today has become ensnared in a legal net which effectively restricts its reach, muzzles its bite, and makes it answerable to a court of law. Accordingly, any examples from late modern military practices must be carefully scrutinized and their inherent disciplinary content distinguished from the artificial legal matrix in which it has become embedded and which preserves it in the midst of a society where the disciplinary mode of control has chiefly given place to the adjudicative mode.

It should be emphasized that the principles which will be enunciated hereunder are not offered as the complete projection or picture of a typical, nor of any particular, disciplinary society in action from day to day in its reality, nor as any statement of rules or practice for the conduct of disciplinary systems. They are to be understood, rather, as theoretical abstractions drawn from the ideas, motivations, purposes, and trends that give meaning and direction to the procedures and sequences actually observed in the reality of disciplinary societies. They are not categorical objectives pursued to achievement whenever possible. They are models or ideals providing standards for the comparison and assessment of actual occurrences, rather than descriptions of actual occurrences.

The discussion which follows is not offered as an exhaustive treatment of the subject. It is intended only as a short introduction sufficient to indicate in the context of the study of the Mixed Court which follows it the nature and degree of the divergencies between Western jurisprudence and the theory of disciplinary systems, and the extent of the almost totally neglected field of disciplinary theory which invites research and inquiry.

WHAT IS DISCIPLINE?

Central to studies of Western jurisprudence lies the theme of law. Unfortunately the applications of the word and the interpretations of the concepts of law have become so wide-ranging, diverse, complex, and numerous that the question, "What is law?" admits of no direct answer. To ask it is merely to invite debate.[1] Central also to Western jurisprudence lies the idea of transcendent, rigid, universal imperatives governing conduct. These are often referred to as *laws*.

In disciplinary theory, by way of contrast, the question, "What is law?" never arises. It is simply irrelevant. Disciplinary theory finds no use for the word *law*, nor for the concept of law, nor for the idea of transcendent, rigid, universal imperatives governing conduct. The answer to the question, "What is discipline?" is not in doubt. Discipline is a state of mind. It is that state of mind which accepts without question the submission of the will and the subordination of the interests of the individual to the will and to the interests of a hierarchical superior in a group. It is the state of mind of the soldier who, when the sergeant orders, "Right turn," immediately turns to the right, without considering for one moment what the sergeant's object may be, nor whether a turn to the left might not be more advantageous. The soldier turns to the right for no other reason than because the sergeant commanded it. It is that state of mind, in the words of Justice Oliver Wendell Holmes, Junior, himself a soldier and a very distinguished lawyer, "which leads a soldier to throw away his life in obedience to a blindly accepted duty, in a cause which he little understands, in a plan of campaign of which he has no notion, under tactics of which he does not see the use."[2]

It is the state of mind of the Ming censor Zuo Guangdou who, unable to prevail upon his emperor, an ineffectual youth, to dismiss evil counselors, wrote, as he lay in unimaginable pain dying of torture inflicted by the emperor's servants, "My body belongs to my ruler-father. I only regret that I have not been able to serve him better."[3]

In a group-hierarchical society there is in every situation a superior and an inferior, and right conduct consists in doing what is commanded by or what will please one's superiors. In the army the private soldier must obey and do what pleases the sergeant. So long as a soldier's conduct is at all times what the sergeant thinks it should be, whether any orders are given or not, life is tolerable. But if the sergeant is displeased, life becomes very uncomfortable and unhappy for the soldier. Similarly, the sergeant must obey and please the lieutenant or the captain, and so on upward to the commander-in-chief.

In traditional Chinese society the superior for the ordinary man was, in family matters, his father; in local community matters, the village elders or local gentry; in business matters, the officers and leaders of his guild; in government matters, the *zhixian*. A woman's superior in all things was, when she was unmarried, her father; when married, her husband; in widowhood, her son.

In a disciplinary society, if any doubt arises as to what should or must be done in a controversial situation, one does not consult any code of law nor go to any lawyer for advice. All that is necessary is simply to ask and get direction from one's immediate superior. There is neither need nor function for any laws or codes of universal imperatives transcending the authority of the immediate superior.

Characteristics of that state of mind which is discipline are further to be discerned in the Chinese concept of *xiao* or the dutiful subordination of a child to a parent's interests, and obedience to the parent's will in all things, sometimes called filial piety. The son, when he differs from his father, accepts without question the reasoning, "I am wrong because I am my father's son; what he says or does is right because he is my father."[4] The projection of this disciplinary state of mind into the body politic is the theme of the *Xiao Jing* and of the Sacred Edicts promulgated by the Ming and Qing emperors for the indoctrination of their subjects. In this teaching, the prime virtue and the first and last duty of every individual is submission and obedience to the authority of status superiors in the hierarchy of the community.

WHAT ARE THE ENDS OF DISCIPLINE?

In jurisprudence the question, "What are the ends and purposes of law?" provokes discussion almost as wide-ranging and diversified as argument over the question, "What is law?" George W. Paton offers as the end of law the development of the intrinsic worth of the human personality by the protection of a cluster of public, social, and private rights and interests, such as national integrity, personal and family liberty and equality, economic security, and so on.[5] It should be noticed in passing that in the value system supported by Western jurisprudence there is present an element of development, improvement, and progress, or at least progression, toward something different and arguably higher in the value scale. Moreover, the system is keyed primarily to the interests of the individual, even when that individual is in conflict with society.

The ends and purposes of discipline, on the other hand, are much more specific, much narrower, much more naive, and very different from the many and complex ideals put forward by different jurists as the ends and purposes of law. They are:

1. The maintenance of the cohesion of the immediate group.
2. The maintenance of the existing hierarchical structure of society.
3. The maintenance of the authority of the superior echelons and the leaders of the group within them.
4. The prevention of change.
5. The preservation and promotion of the interests of the group in an environment of warring or contending groups.

The element of development or progression into something different is not present in the value scale but is negatived, and the system is designed to protect the interests of the group, not those of the individual. The maxim of jurisprudence, *Fiat justitia ruat coelum* (Let Justice be done though the heavens should fall), is anathema in disciplinary theory. In disciplinary systems the object is to prevent the heavens from falling at all costs, to preserve and maintain the status quo even at the sacrifice of individual interests.

In the military context this principle was bluntly expressed by John

Henry Wigmore when he said: "The prime object of military organization is Victory not Justice. . . . If [the army] can do justice to its men, well and good. But Justice is always secondary and Victory is always primary."[6] In 1948 General Eisenhower, addressing a meeting of lawyers, said:

> I would like to call your attention to one fact about the Army—about the Armed Services. It was never set up to ensure justice. It is set up as your servant to do a particular job and . . . that function demands a violation of the very concepts upon which our government is established.[7]

Rule in Japan under the Tokugawa shoguns may be classified as a disciplinary system. The case of the succession to the fief of Echigo is instructive. Wigmore relates the facts thus:

> The incumbent *daimyo,* Mitsunaga, was childless and one of the two seneschals intrigued with the lord's brother, Nagayori, to have the son of the latter adopted as heir to the title and the fief; while the other seneschal used his efforts against this step and to gain his purposes brought the matter to the attention of the *shogun.* The latter looked upon the inability to come to an agreement as seditious in its tendencies, especially in a quarter when only the example of peace and smoothness should be set, and the decision was that the *daimyo* and his brother should be exiled with the complaining seneschal while the other intriguer was to be put to death and the fief confiscated. No doubt jealousy of the power of this large fief was one of the elements in this particular decision.[8]

In this result the harmony and cohesion of the group and the consolidation, confirmation, and extension of the authority and power of the superior, the shogun, took precedence over a just settlement of the dispute according to the merits and in the interests of the individual parties. So also at the level of the schoolroom, if two children quarrel over the possession of an apple, the school principal may punish them both for fighting and give the apple to another child or pocket it and take it home for dinner.

Successful leaders, nevertheless, are aware that the doing of "justice," that is, what will satisfy their followers' sense of values, can be very advantageous in maintaining the cohesion, obedience, and confidence of the group, and this becomes especially important when the leaders' authority is weak or their hold on it tenuous. Thus in Japan when Yoritomo, and after him the Hojo, were struggling to establish and maintain hegemony against the competition of other powerful groups—including that of the imperial court itself—they took care to offer their followers a high standard of dispute resolution according to the values of the day. The result was the "robust and stern justice" of the courts of the Kamakura *bakufu* that secured the confidence of the unruly warriors and did much to stabilize unrest and ensure the acceptance and support of the regime.[9]

So also in China, in the Yuan period, when the Mongol conquerors were heavily outnumbered and somewhat uncertain of their grip, they provided very fair tribunals for the enforcement of discipline and for dispute resolution.[10]

INSUBORDINATION, CRIME, AND PUNISHMENT

In jurisprudence much space is given to the consideration and analysis of the concepts of crime, criminal law, and the punishment of criminal behavior. Crime is regarded as an offense against society, and the seriousness of an offense is measured by the degree of its criminality. The basis of criminality is a moral lapse—a lapse from the standards of behavior generally acceptable and observed as proper in the community for the time being, and expressed in and required by a rigid, universal, and comprehensive code of rules.

In disciplinary theory, crime and criminal sanctions receive no consideration at all, but much attention is devoted to insubordination and its treatment. In a disciplinary system, deviant behavior is not regarded as an offense against society, but as a private matter for adjustment between the parties affected—unless it amounts to insubordination or disobedience of orders, threatens the authority of superiors in the hierarchy of command, or is deemed by the leaders of the group to be prejudicial to their policies. Only in such a case does it call for notice and remedial action by the group leaders as a breakdown in discipline.

In an adjudicative system, the adjudicator exercises powers of punishment limited to those specifically designated in a transcendent code and only for those offenses specifically defined in the code, upon a principle of *nulla poena sine lege* (No penalty [shall be imposed] unless there is a law [authorizing it]). This principle is expressed in the fifth amendment to the Constitution of the United States (1791) in the words, "No person . . . shall be deprived of life, liberty, or property without due process of law." An early prototype is found in the Magna Carta (1215) in the words, "No freeman shall be arrested or imprisoned or deprived of his land or ruined . . . except by the lawful judgment of his peers or by the law of the land."

In a disciplinary system, on the other hand, the authority at the apex of command (e.g. the commander-in-chief in any army or the emperor in China) possesses the power to repress and to punish, by any means and to any extent, any action that is regarded by that authority as improper, displeasing, or prejudicial to the regime.

The Emperor Kangxi (K'ang-hsi) has left sufficient record of his own thoughts to afford us an insight into the working of his mind as he went about the exercise of these powers. His thoughts ran along these lines:

> Giving life to people and killing people—those are the powers that the emperor has. . . . The Board of Punishments recommended that Hu [a cruel and rapacious official] be dismissed and sent into exile for three years. I ordered instead that he be executed with his family and in his native place so that all the local gentry might learn how I regarded such behavior. . . . The commander-in-chief reported that Colonel Malangga had fled; and after Prince Cani verified this in his secret report, I had Malangga beheaded. . . . But apart from . . . men like those who plotted against me in the Heir-Apparent crisis and had to be killed immediately and secretly without trial, I have been merciful where possible.[11]

In practice the plenary powers of punishment possessed by the high command in disciplinary systems are usually delegated for convenience to subordinate staff officers and administrators, but only within specific limits and subject to detailed instructions as to their exercise. In China, for instance, the sixth division of the *Da Qing Lu Li* comprised a code of such instructions addressed to disciplinary administrators.[12] But the powers of punishment themselves are unlimited and extend to all actions displeasing to authority whether specifically made punishable or not. This is one of the distinguishing marks by which a disciplinary system may be identified. In the British army tradition, all disciplinary officers and tribunals were, and in some cases still are, empowered to punish "conduct to the prejudice of good order and military discipline."[13] In China the *zhixian* or district surrogate for discipline (and his superiors in the chain of command) were authorized and expected to punish anybody who did "what ought not to be done" even if no punishment for such an act was prescribed in the schedule of authorized punishments comprising the *Da Qing Lu Li*.[14]

PENOLOGY AND REEDUCATION

In legal theory there is room for much discussion and difference of opinion as to the ends and purposes of punishment. They are seen as complex, changing progressively as society itself evolves and progresses. Nevertheless it may be affirmed that in legal systems, at least in the recent past, punishments have been intended, broadly, to mark society's disapproval of the moral lapse, to deter the criminal and other potential criminals from any such lapses in the future, to isolate offenders from society by confinement, at least for a time, in a place where they can do no more harm, and to reform their moral characters. In disciplinary theory the prime objectives are quite different and much simpler, and they do not change. The approach is one of correcting insubordination and restoring discipline in the group rather than of punishing individuals for crime. In disciplinary theory, deviance is not thought of as a criminal offense but as a disorderly offense.[15] Its treatment is didactic and educative rather than penal.[16] Its one purpose above all others is to reestablish in the consciousness of the group to which the offender belongs, as well as in the offender's own mind, those conditions of unqualified respect for superior authority and unquestioning obedience to the will of superiors which is discipline. The crude methods of physical torture which were used to this end in imperial times have largely given way in modern China to far more sophisticated and more directly effective psychological reconditioning procedures.[17]

If an offender is not responsive to treatment, the ultimate sanctions are denial of the benefits of membership in the group and expulsion, friendless and alone, into a hostile world, as when an unruly student is expelled from school, an army officer is drummed out of the regiment, or a Christian king is excommunicated for defiance of the authority of the Church. In bad cases, or where expulsion is not likely to prove effective, the offender is sometimes simply destroyed as a threat to the survival of the group or to the security of its leaders.

COLLECTIVE PUNISHMENT

Western jurisprudence demands, as a general rule subject to few and minor exceptions, that no person should be punished for another's crime, and great care is taken to isolate and identify the actual offender. Disciplinary theory, on the other hand, regards as advantageous and often requires that punishment and remedial action consequent upon an act of insubordination or disobedience should extend beyond the actual offender to the other members of the immediate group. It is not essential that the particular offender should be found nor only the offender punished.

The principle of collective responsibility and punishment of a whole group for the insubordination of some of the individual members of it has been used consistently in disciplinary systems of rule from Ham murabi to Stalin.[18] It was used extensively and for many years successfully in China to ensure order by the application of the *bao jia* system, which divided the population into groups of five or ten households, making all the households in the group equally responsible for the good conduct of each and punishable for the delicts of any of them. But the principle of collective responsibility was general, in varying applications, throughout China's history. In a memorial of 179 B.C. the principle is referred to as being "of ancient origin."[19] It prevailed in Han times and continued to do so until the fall of the Manzhou dynasty in 1912.[20] The *Da Qing Lu Li* for example contained specific instructions that, in cases of high treason, not only was the guilty party to be executed, but most near relatives, male and female, were also to be executed or reduced to slavery.[21]

General Sir Gerald Templer used the principle effectively in Malaya to repress insurgency during the emergency conditions of 1948–60. The measures he took were severe and proved very effective in restoring the minds of the villagers and townspeople to a state of high respect for himself personally and unquestioning obedience and submission to his will.[22]

SELECTIVE PUNISHMENT

Collective punishment is punishment of the many for the offenses of the few, so that the innocent as well as the guilty suffer. In disciplinary systems the converse is also acceptable—the few may be punished for the sins of the many, so that some of the guilty go free. Decimation in the ancient Roman army is an example. When it was desired to punish a specific body of troops for mutiny or some other gross dereliction of duty committed collectively, one man in ten was taken from the group and clubbed or stoned to death. The men selected for execution were chosen by lot, irrespective of each man's personal culpability in the affair.[23] Decimation was still practiced in the British Army as late as the seventeenth century.[24] Sometimes a commander would destroy the whole offending group, not by putting all the members of it to death, but by the device of abolishing it as a unit and sending the former members to serve in a number of other, better behaved units.

SUBSTITUTIVE PUNISHMENT

In the Chinese disciplinary system it was not always regarded as necessary to punish the actual offender even when correctly identified. So long as someone was prepared to undergo the punishment, the offender might in some cases be allowed to go free. Thus in imperial times a son, grandson, or younger brother was often allowed to assume a punishment imposed upon his father or hierarchical superior so that the latter went free. In some periods this practice was institutionalized by official regulation and allowed even in capital cases.[25] Such forms of substituted punishment are perfectly acceptable in disciplinary theory. In disciplinary systems the purposes of punishment are directed ultimately to the reeducation of the group in attitudes of subordination to superiors. An important example of the proper attitudes is filial piety. How better could the principles of filial piety be inculcated and emphasized than by allowing and encouraging a son to give his life to save his father's even when his father deserves to lose his life?

The regular application of the principles of collective, selective, and substitutive punishment in disciplinary systems, and the general revulsion from these procedures in adjudicative ones, illustrate and confirm the divergencies we have noticed between the ends of the respective systems and between the types of remedial action adopted. In adjudicative systems the essence of the process lies in the identification of the individual culprit and the infliction of penal sanctions for the wrongdoing upon that individual alone, and the action is taken in the interests of the other members of the society individually. In disciplinary systems the essence of the process lies in the restoration of a firm state of hierarchical submission and discipline in the group where it has broken down, and action is taken in the interests of the group collectively and of its leaders. This is achieved by the application of pains and penalties and reeducative processes, not only to the culprit individually, but also to other members of the subgroup of relatives or associates of which the chief offender forms part. In extreme cases the remedy may lie in the complete eradication of the whole subgroup where the lapse occurred. The identification and punishment of the actual offender is only a collateral and incidental part of this process and is not always insisted upon nor achieved. It is often sufficient for the maintenance of discipline and the suppression of insubordination that inferior ranks should be made aware and kept aware that upon any insubordination occurring someone, if not the whole group, is certain to be punished for it and swiftly, whether the right person or not.

When the present writer was a boy at school the application of this principle in the classroom was well recognized. When an offense was committed in class while the master's back was turned so that he could not tell who did it, it was his practice to call upon the boy responsible to confess, and if no one confessed, then the master would cane the whole class, the innocent with the guilty. None of the boys and none of the parents took any exception to this procedure, which was regarded as perfectly normal, just, and proper. It played an effective part in maintaining a high standard of behavior in class and a high respect for the master and his commands.

USE OF THE AMNESTY

An important part in the maintenance of the disciplinary state of mind lies in fostering the notion that the high command is omnipotent—not only can it punish at will but it can release from punishment with equal facility. Hence the use by some Chinese emperors of the amnesty as a device to impress the idea that the emperor could not only take away but give also, if and when he was pleased to do so. It served to enhance substantially the awe and majesty of the emperor's omnipotence and to lend color to his "father and mother" image. It taught that in disciplinary systems rewards flow to lower ranks when superior ranks are happy and content and have cause to celebrate.[26]

DISCIPLINARY TRIBUNALS

In jurisprudence much space is given to judges, magistrates, courts of justice, litigation, trials, prosecuting and defending counsel, and all the principles, techniques, and procedures of adjudicatory processes of decision, particularly those designed to ensure fairness and impartiality. These receive no mention in disciplinary theory, but there will be found in their place discussion of disciplinary tribunals, disciplinary officers, investigations, inquisitions, inquiries, public castigation ceremonies, and so on. Tribunals are not limited to evidence given openly in court. They may inform themselves by secret agents or in any way they choose. They are neither impartial nor independent, but are delegates of the high command, and their prime duty is to further the interests of their commander. These are often, but by no means always, identified with the interests of the group and best served by being fair to the individuals who comprise the group. The maxim, "No man shall be judge in his own cause" is negatived. Authority in a disciplinary system must always be judge in its own cause. The principle that an accused person is to be deemed innocent until proved guilty is negatived.[27] The mere fact of arrest is evidence enough that the prisoner has displeased authority in some way, and the onus is on the accused to provide a valid excuse, correct this situation, and get back somehow into the good graces of superior authority. The fact of arrest also indicates that those in authority have taken the view that the prisoner has committed the offense, and to plead not guilty may only increase the punishment. It may amount to contradicting the disciplinary surrogate, the delegate of the high command, face to face—a very serious insubordination.[28] The literature of imperial China affords graphic examples. "How dare you deny your guilt?" demands the disciplinary surrogate of the perfectly innocent accused in Wu Ching-tzu's novel *The Scholars*.[29]

There is perhaps no more obvious and significant contrast between adjudicative and disciplinary systems in practice than the presence and crucial importance in adjudicative systems of an independent bench and bar not subject to direction by superior authority, and the total absence of any such features in disciplinary systems.

JURISDICTION AND COMPETENCE

In jurisprudence a court's authority and effectiveness are restrained, and it must hold its hand if it is without jurisdiction. The concept of jurisdiction is a creature of legal systems, and whether a court has jurisdiction or not is a question of law. The concept has no place and is not used in disciplinary systems. A somewhat analogous, but very different, concept in disciplinary systems is that of competence. The competence of a disciplinary tribunal is simply the extent of its ability to ensure the physical enforcement of its own orders. This is a question of fact, not a question of law. If in fact a disciplinary tribunal can compel obedience to its orders, then it has competence and nothing more is required for the validity of its judgments. The extent of a disciplinary tribunal's competence, that is the authority and effectiveness of its decrees, is ultimately limited to the extent of the authority of the high command of which it is the delegate, and to the area of effectiveness of that high command's orders.

COMMAND STANDING ORDERS

In jurisprudence much importance is attached to laws, statutes, acts, legislation, bylaws, statutory regulations, and similar abiding rules of universal application. Indeed the whole system turns upon the existence, the interpretation, and the observance of transcendent rules, that is to say predetermined rigid imperatives transcending the parties, the government officials, and the tribunal itself, and binding on them all.

There is no place for such rules and they receive no mention in disciplinary theory, but much is said about command standing orders, routine orders, local standing orders, staff instructions, schedules of duties, directives, and so on. Dissemination of these is not, as a rule, to the general public—they are primarily intended for the information and direction of administrative officers, who will inform their hierarchical inferiors of anything that it is necessary for them to know.

In the narrow circles of the lesser disciplinary communities of the nursery, the schoolroom, and the family there is often no need for any written rules of behavior at all. On the other hand in a very large disciplinary polity with a specific identity persisting over a long period of time, such as the Chinese Empire or the British Army, the maintenance of discipline and the enforcement of the commander's will call for the agency of an extensive network of administrative and of executive officials, and their work must be regularized and coordinated. In such cases there tends to arise in time, out of the constant repetition of similar action in similar circumstances in an almost static social structure, a pattern of conventions, customs, traditions, and regularities in the application of disciplinary enforcement procedures. These, so far as they may be acceptable to the high command, are often encouraged for the sake of the convenience and help they afford in the smooth running of the administration. They become widely known and generally accepted and are sometimes embodied with other directives in a code of instructions or standing orders, or perhaps a schedule of punishments issued by headquarters for observance by administrators and disciplinary officials in the uniform execution of their duties.

Such was the basic nature of the administrative codes issued by the dynastic rulers of China from the Tang code to the *Da Qing Lu Li*. Such also was the basic nature of the codes called articles of war often issued by army commanders in Europe and America in the seventeenth to the nineteenth centuries.

It is very necessary to distinguish carefully such standing orders of a commander in a disciplinary system from the transcendent, rigid, universal imperatives for the control of conduct upon which Western jurisprudence is founded. The two are quite different in nature, concept, meaning, and purpose, and it is very unfortunate that by a process akin to the backward translation which we have previously discussed they should both sometimes come to be labeled with the same nametag, "laws."

But our chief concern here is not with names, definitions of words, or semantics. We are concerned to distinguish two different types of rules, and the different functions of those types, in the machinery of two different systems of order. In one of these, which we have called the *adjudicative* or *legal* system, norms of behavior, reduced to transcendent, rigid, universal imperatives for the control of conduct, provide the pivot and the center upon which all turns and from which all hangs. "Primary rules of obligation are the heart and centre of a legal system," says H. L. A. Hart.[30] Legal systems have their origin in the cosmological idea, peculiar to Western thought, of bringing about order from outside the chaos, through the control of conduct by the transcendent rigid imperatives of an omnipotent power external to the nexus.

In the other system of order, which we have called *disciplinary*, standing conduct directives or rules, if found at all, are of internal origin, used for convenience and uniformity only, variable according to the internal circumstances of each case, and completely malleable in the hands of the authority who issued them, and who may choose to follow the rule, alter it, or ignore it at will, according to the circumstances of each individual case. Generally, of course, commanders, for the sake of consistency and stability of administration, will decline to depart from regularities and will make a practice of following the rules. This was the case in China where the emperor generally followed his own dynastic code of punishments, but where it was quite possible for him to ignore the code and do whatever he himself felt right, if he wanted to.[31] Similarly the board of punishments was quite able to recommend action contrary to, or outside, the code if it saw fit. There existed no machinery, whether by way of a supreme court or otherwise, and no concept of any machinery, designed to compel restraint at the suit of an inferior upon the emperor, the board, or any superior, and there was no notion in Chinese thought that any such compellable restraint might be possible or even desirable.

A further significant difference in the nature and function of rules in the machinery of the two systems may be noted. In an adjudicative system it is of the essence that the predetermined rules should be matters of public knowledge. Everyone is afforded means of knowing them and everyone is presumed to know them. In a disciplinary system, however, secret rules are possible and acceptable—that is to say there may be valid rules that are known only to the commander and to the delegate, the local administrator, yet they will be determinative in any case to which the delegate may apply them. Thus in the disciplinary system of Tokugawa Japan, the *Kujikata Osadamegaki* put into force by the Shogun Yoshimune in 1742 and containing, among other things, a corpus of behavioral standards and rules of general application, was, in its concept, a secret document.[32] It constituted a manual of instructions to senior disciplinary commissioners for their use in the administration of order and was intended for their eyes only. It contained within itself the injunction, "Except for the Commissioners, this is not to be seen by anyone," and this restriction was intended by the high command, the shogun, to apply to the whole contents of the manual.[33] Yet its provisions could be determinative in any case to which the disciplinary commissioner might see fit to apply them. Such secrecy is not at all repugnant to the concept of determinative rules in disciplinary theory. Of course the contents of the *Osadamegaki* could not in practice remain a close secret for very long, but in theory and in concept its nature remained for a hundred years at least that of a secret communication from the high command to its delegates, the disciplinary officials. In 1841 a bannerman, Ōno Kennojō, was arrested and punished for violating its secrecy by publishing a copy of it.[34]

In China as late as 1930, we find the Shanghai District Court acting on a secret order issued by the Nationalist government to the courts establishing a rule that persons charged with offenses involving communist activities were not to be tried in the civil courts according to regular procedure but were to be handed over to the military authorities to be dealt with in military courts. This raised the problem for the Foreign Office, thinking in terms of Western jurisprudence, as to whether such secret orders were or were not "laws of China" within the meaning of the international agreement setting up the district court.[35]

In China the "quantitative overlap of authority by regularity" of administration never reached the point where the rules solidified into anything more concrete than the formalized instructions of superior authority, capable of being superseded in any particular case by other instructions if one went high enough in the chain of command.[36] In China substantive law never became "secreted in the interstices of procedure."[37]

In military systems also it may be observed that never does any conventional procedure, any custom of the service, or any tradition overrule the commander's discretion to depart from it if he wants to. In practice, nevertheless, commanders generally find it convenient and helpful to follow well-worn paths and familiar sequences and to uphold their own orders.

CONTRACT

In jurisprudence the concept of contract is of major significance. Upon it are founded the vast and complex structures of rights and obligations that govern and control buying and selling, lending and leasing, banking, insurance, companies, and all the multifarious transactions of industry, trade, and commerce, as well as many aspects of family and personal life. The law of contract is a highly technical subject but for our purposes it is sufficient to describe a contract, in Western law, as being essentially an agreement which either of the parties may enforce, horizontally as it were, against the other, in the courts, as of right.

In this sense the concept of contract is unknown in disciplinary theory. In disciplinary systems of order there may be found agreements in plenty, and they often look very like Western contracts, but they are agreements which never ripen into contract. They remain promises merely. They never embody the idea of enforcement as of right which is the basis of contract. In disciplinary theory no one ever has any right to insist upon the observance of an agreement. The utmost that an aggrieved party can do by way of enforcement through official government channels is to go vertically upward and ask the superior of the other party, as of grace, to issue a command vertically downward, directing the defaulter to honor the agreement. The superior has an unfettered discretion to grant or to refuse the suppliant this favor, but in either case is quite likely to punish both parties for quarreling and for not settling their quarrels without disturbing higher authority.

It follows that in Chinese thinking an agreement or a promise never crystallizes into a fixed and unalterable code of obligation. Agreements and promises remain no more than statements of present intention. If circumstances change and they become difficult, irksome, or unprofitable for either party to fulfil, the other party cannot resist a reopening of the negotiations and a substitution of less onerous terms.

CUSTOM

Adjudicative or legal systems of order being egalitarian and not hierarchical in principle, the individual when in doubt as to what course of action to take in a difficult situation does not go to a superior for orders but to a lawyer for advice, and the lawyer consults that corpus of fixed and universal imperatives which is the basis and sine qua non of adjudicative systems. It follows that the codes and sets of imperatives must be, and in practice are, very extensive, touching upon almost every aspect of the social behavior, social activities, and interpersonal relations of human beings.

In disciplinary theory the situation is quite different. In disciplinary systems it is possible and indeed to be expected that large areas of social relationships will be left almost totally outside the control system of the high command to regulate themselves according to common sense, local custom, fashion, and tradition. Such is the case with matters of family concern, of marriage, divorce, and inheritance, matters of trade, commerce, and business, of partnership, of bills of exchange, of weights and measures. In general, notice is taken of such matters only so far as may be deemed necessary or advisable in order to preserve and enhance cohesion in the group, the unquestioned authority of its leaders, and the prosecution of its leaders' objectives for the time being. Thus in a military system the commander will not be concerned at all with a soldier's matrimonial, family, or business affairs except so far as may be necessary to keep the soldier content, with high morale and a spirit fit for battle. In the disciplinary system of China, irrelevant matters of family, business, and trade were left for oversight, management, and decision chiefly to the care of the groups wherein they arose—the family, the guild, or the village. Imperial concern in such matters was chiefly directed to the upholding of the ideals of *xiao* or filial subordination and of the unquestioning obedience of status inferiors to superiors in all circumstances.

Hence the absence of any comprehensive civil or commercial code or code of family obligations in traditional China. Hence the meager and merely sidelong references to such matters as marriage and divorce and inheritance in dynastic codes of administrative instructions to officials, such as the *Da Qing Lu Li*. Hence also the notorious lack of uniformity in currency standards, mercantile practices, and weights and measures. Guilds, trades, and local groups were free to fix their own standards in all such matters, and customarily they did.

TERRITORIAL SOVEREIGNTY

In Western theory, at least since the Peace of Westphalia in 1648, territorial limitations have been at the heart of the concept of a state and its rulers.[38] Subject to some exceptions that need not concern us here, the authority of the rulers of a sovereign state over everybody and everything within the territorial limits of their home state is total. Their authority over any person or any thing within the territorial limits of a foreign state is nil. In disciplinary theory on the other hand territorial sovereignty is unknown. Territorial boundaries, if they exist at all, are not permanent—they are temporary and for convenience only. Authority is not limited territorially. It is personal and applies to persons subject to it wherever they may be found. A picturesque illustration of the inconsequence of territorial boundaries is offered by David J. Steinberg and his coauthors, who write:

> The inconclusive Vietnamese-Lao wars of the seventeenth century, for example, were resolved when the Lê Emperor in Vietnam and the Lao king agreed that every inhabitant in the upper Mekong valley who lived in a house built on stilts owed allegiance to Laos, while those whose homes had earth floors owed allegiance to Vietnam.[39]

The authority of army commanders over their troops is the same when they are in a foreign country as it is at home.[40] Their authority may sometimes be limited territorially, as when a general is appointed to command in one of several different theaters of war or a colonel is given responsibility for the defense of a limited area or section of the front. Such limitations however are not political and not permanent. They are for convenience of operation only and are liable to change at any time.

DISPUTE RESOLUTION

In Western jurisprudence it is seen as the function of the state to provide adequate machinery for the prompt resolution of citizens' disputes according to the appropriate provisions of the corpus of fixed imperatives upon which the system rests. Every citizen has access to this machinery and may set it in motion at will. A citizen who succeeds in a claim is entitled as of right to call in aid the monopoly of force possessed by the state in order to compel payment and satisfaction of the claim in accordance with the order of the court.

In disciplinary theory no such considerations arise and no such machinery is necessary. Inferior ranks are forbidden to quarrel, and if they do it is the duty of their immediate superiors to stifle the dissension at its source and prevent it from troubling any of the officials of the high command.

Where discipline prevails all jural processes are didactic. Dispute resolution is always the responsibility of hierarchical superiors, who are expected to instruct their inferiors, the contending parties, in their duty not to quarrel, and are expected to settle the dispute so as to maintain discipline and the status quo. They are expected to act in the interests of the group and according to all the surrounding circumstances, rather than simply according to the merits as between the parties.

The vast majority of disputes in precommunist China were smothered and disposed of in this way at the level of the group in which they arose.[41] The process of such disposal is often referred to as mediation, or better, as didactic conciliation.[42] The process has been authoritatively described and analyzed.[43] It tended to favor the strong at the expense of the weak. An aggrieved party who was bold enough, or desperate enough, could petition the local district surrogate for discipline seeking redress, and there was always a trickle of unfortunates who did this. Whether the surrogate took any action, and what action he took, depended largely on the identity of the parties, the political implications of the quarrel, the effect it might have on his own future, and other extraneous circumstances.

The arbitrary attitudes of disciplinary officials toward petitions may be examined in the context of the Mixed Court of the International Settlement at Shanghai in 1911, when the consuls took control of its proceedings. H. F. Handley-Derry, the senior British assessor of the day, reporting on it to his consul-general, said:

> There are certain petitions which are refused without a colour of right, but in the majority there is some reason given for refusing, and in this refusal one finds invariably the deeply rooted idea of making the two parties come to some amicable arrangement, in which the official takes as little part as possible. . . . Formerly where the defendant was a man of substance the Magistrate, as often as not, would refuse to issue a summons and would order the plaintiff to go to the defendant again and try to settle the case without recourse to litigation. If the defendant still refused to settle the matter the plaintiff might be prevented entirely from getting satisfaction, or the Magistrate might again try to persuade the defendant to settle.[44]

The paternal and disciplinary nature of the approach to dispute resolution in China is revealed in the endorsements made by the Mixed Court magistrate upon petitions when rejecting them. For example, one such endorsement reads:

> As you say in your petition, Liu Wen-tzou is a respectable merchant. Why should he delay payment of, or try to deny liability for whatever is still owing on the price of the work? The best thing is for you to go to him again and ask for payment. You must not create disturbances and lawsuits. Receipt attached returned herewith.[45]

Another one reads: "I will write to the Canton guild again telling them to settle the matter promptly, but you must not be obstinate and prolong the lawsuit so as to bring trouble on yourself."[46]

In disciplinary systems if a superior authority hears a petition for redress of a grievance at all, it is heard as a matter of grace, never as a matter of right. In particular, redress of wrongs done by superiors to inferiors is always discretionary, never a right, and claims for it must always be brought in the first place to the superior claimed against.

In disciplinary theory it is not helpful to try making any distinction between civil and criminal process. Proceedings before the disciplinary officer whatever their nature are always directed to the same object: restoration of harmony and discipline by the punishment and reeducation of those responsible for disturbing it.

The principle of *res judicata* (a matter on which judgment has been passed), that is to say the principle that once an issue has been decided by a competent court it is decided for all time and cannot again be disputed between the same parties in any subsequent proceedings, is familiar in jurisprudence but is negatived in disciplinary theory. It is always open to a disciplinary officer to reconsider some question that has already been decided and settled, and to come to a different conclusion and give a different decision.[47]

The principle of *stare decisis et non quieta movere* (abide by the decided cases and do not stir up questions that have been put to rest), by which, in common-law systems, inferior courts are bound to follow precedents established in the decisions of superior courts, is negatived in disciplinary systems. A commander's discretion must never be trammelled by anything that may have taken place on any previous occasion.[48]

In jurisprudence the transcendent, rigid, universal imperatives of conduct, which are the foundation of a legal order and upon which the whole structure rests, override and control the direction of affairs by all lesser authorities and rule-makers. In disciplinary systems on the contrary the orders and directions of the immediate leaders of the local group are more efficacious and are obeyed in preference to the rules and regulations of the more remote political power.

Thus if a military officer orders a body of troops to march down a city street the soldiers will obey and march. They will not stop to consider the traffic regulations which provide that pedestrians shall walk on the footpath and not along the carriageway. Particular instances of the operation of this factor in the Chinese system of order will be noticed in later chapters.[49] For a further Chinese illustration, the house-rules of the *tsu*, or extended family, of Wu, in Jiangsu may be instanced.[50] It is clear from a study of these rules that even as late as 1933 the efficacy of the provisions of the civil code and the legislation generally of the Nationalist government of China depended, in the group constituted by the Wu family, on the extent to which the officials of the *tsu* were prepared to accept and give effect to them.

In Western society this principle of disciplinary theory proves useful in throwing light upon certain aspects of trade unionism which do not respond to interpretation in terms of legal theory. Thus in the English case of *Gouriet v. Union of Post Office Workers and Others*[51] it appeared that the executive council of the union had resolved to call upon its members not to handle mail to or from the Republic of South Africa. This ban, if put into force, would amount to a serious criminal offense—willfully obstructing and hindering the delivery of Her Majesty's mails. A private citizen took action in the courts to restrain the union by injunction from so flouting the law. It was objected that the action could not proceed without the consent of the attorney-general, and the attorney-general refused to consent. The Court of Appeal however allowed the action to proceed. The court held that any citizen was entitled to come to the court and ask that the law be enforced. The attorney-general could not by his veto negate the force of the criminal law. "Be you never so high, the law is above you," thundered Lord Denning. Trade unions, he said, are not above the law and it is the duty of the Court of Appeal to uphold the law.[52] The House of Lords, however, declined to underwrite Lord Denning's rhetoric and reversed the Court of Appeal, holding that the attorney-general's discretion was unassailable and that since he had refused consent the action could not proceed and there was no more to be said.[53]

In all the disputation, however, none of the argument went to the heart of the matter, which was simply that the union was thinking in terms of a disciplinary system of order and Lord Denning was thinking in terms of a legal system. In disciplinary theory the leaders of the group are obeyed at all cost, notwithstanding what more remote authorities may say or do. Here in this case was an example in the West of the same problem that so bedeviled the Mixed Court at Shanghai, the problem of how to find a common ground upon which to reconcile, not differing concepts of law, but differing concepts of order, the disciplinary and the legal.

This is a perennial problem in trade unionism. In Australia in 1983 a trade union directed its members not to answer questions put to them at a certain royal commission. The commissioner said that "the union had indicated by its actions that it considered it was above the law."[54] It is suggested however that a more perceptive and more productive approach to the union attitude is to look at it in terms of disciplinary theory, where no question arises of being above or below the law. The whole concept of law is simply irrelevant. It is a different system of order. In many aspects trade union practice responds better to interpretation in terms of group-disciplinary, rather than legal, systems of order. Thus, for one example, the ultimate penalty for deviance is that of a group-disciplinary system—expulsion from the group to fend for yourself in a hostile world.

DISCIPLINE AND THE RULE OF FORCE

Disciplinary systems are to be sharply distinguished from the "Oriental Despotism" and the "Rule by Terror" of Karl A. Wittfogel,[55] the gunman gangster situation, the pure domination-submission model, and all those systems where execution of the leader's will depends primarily on force. The success of a disciplinary system depends on the maintenance of a state of mind, not on the application or the threat of force. Force only becomes relevant when that state of mind breaks down. The Duke of Wellington emphasized this when he was giving evidence before a royal commission on punishments in the British Army in 1836. He referred to the state of discipline in the army he commanded at the end of the Peninsular War and said, "When I quitted that army upon the Garonne I do not think it was possible to see anything in a higher state of discipline; and I believe there was a total discontinuance of all punishment."[56]

The disciplinary state is not a mere domination of the weak by the strong. It is something far more complex.[57] It always involves a mutual relationship of dependency between superior and inferior and, to a greater or lesser degree, a mutual relationship of respect.[58]

It should be noted further that the state of mind upon which discipline depends can be, and often is, very acceptable and agreeable to those experiencing it. Life under a system of discipline if the leadership is good can be relaxing, rewarding, and emotionally very satisfying in every rank of the hierarchy. It is not necessarily an oppressive system, although it may appear oppressive to a person who has been conditioned never to think otherwise than in terms of the rights-conscious and freedom-conscious values of the legal system of the West. It is much easier, of course, for a disciplinary system than for a legal system to degenerate into oppression and a rule of force. Disciplinary systems depend for their success, far more than legal systems do, upon the personal caliber of those administering them.

It should be made clear, perhaps, at this point that it is not the purpose of this work to make or to infer any comparative value judgments between the two systems. We are not concerned here with which is "better" according to any scale of values. The intention is simply to make the point that one cannot attain to a realistic understanding of what goes on in one system by regarding it and trying to interpret it in terms of the other.

If the submissions made in this work so far have any validity, then an answer to the methodological problem of how, and in what terms, faithfully to discuss Chinese systems of dispute resolution and of order maintenance begins to appear. It would seem that the Western mind must first be purged utterly of all it ever held of law and jurisprudence and retrained to learn instead how to think, feel, and express itself in terms of, and against a background of, discipline and the principles of the science of disciplinary theory. Jean Escarra foreshadowed this when he wrote in 1936 that the Chinese had their own conception of law "qu'on ne peut saisir qu'en faisant à peu prés table rasé des theories occidentales sur le sujet" (which one cannot grasp except by wiping the slate almost entirely clean of Western theories on the subject).[59]

This might not be at all easy for a Western lawyer to do. Can a leopard change his spots? "The thinking habits of centuries as well as the individual perfecting of this craft over a lifetime make it difficult if not impossible for most lawyers to think in any other way" than in terms of universal compulsive rules, says R. W. M. Dias.[60] But this is precisely what is called for in disciplinary theory. George W. Paton, thinking in terms of jurisprudence, wrote, "It is hard to conceive of a duty unless there is a corresponding right."[61] But this is exactly what must be done if one is to work in terms of disciplinary theory, in which duties without corresponding rights are of the essence. Early in the history of the Western intrusion into the East a grave difficulty arose in trying to communicate in terms of legal rights. There was no word in the Chinese or Japanese language to express the idea until words were invented and assigned for the purpose.[62]

André Bonnichon commented on the difficulty that meets the Western jurist (including himself) in any attempt "to grasp a clear picture of a system so far removed from that with which he is familiar and even from that which he believes possible."[63] He wrote that the basic conceptions of the system are not to be obtained from any texts and he was compelled to draw his understanding of them from his own personal experiences over twenty-three years in China, both as a free man and as a prisoner.[64]

The Western lawyer's problem with disciplinary theory is not merely one of reasoning in a different way. It is a problem of perception, not of ratiocination. The lawyer must become accommodated to moving in a different world of discourse.

Discipline is at least as much a matter of emotional conviction as it is of intellectual thinking. A disciplined soldier develops a special attitude to command, coming to live with it, accept it, and respect it "as he does the force of gravity or the march of time."[65] Under a Western legal system, lawyer and client may be able intellectually to accept that the wisest course is to do what a hierarchical superior, say the Supreme Court of the United States, says they must, because no further appeal is available to them under the rules. But the same lawyer and client would probably find it very difficult to feel convinced in their hearts that no other course is ever possible than to do what a superior commands because, and for no other reason than because, the superior says so. Yet that *feeling* is the basic foundation upon which discipline rests, discipline being, as we have seen, a state of mind. In this view, legal scholarship, a "trained legal mind," and many years of habitually thinking in terms of the transcendental rigid imperatives of Western jurisprudence may appear as serious handicaps rather than as aids to understanding.[66] A. F. P. Hulsewé tells us that when he undertook his classic studies and translations of Han law he had no "grounding in any system of law," ancient or modern, had never studied any such subject, and deliberately refrained from doing so lest he might misinterpret the Chinese material by putting alien constructions upon it.[67]

What sort of results do we get if we apply a disciplinary interpretation to the Chinese scene? It will be instructive to examine first the so-called district magistrate and second the Mixed Court of the International Settlement at Shanghai, and to compare the pictures they offer in terms of disciplinary theory with the showing they make in terms of conventional legal systems.

CHAPTER 3

The District Magistrate

Consider that familiar figure of sinological literature, the district magistrate, "dispensing justice" in judicial proceedings by regularly and as a matter of course beating innocent parties and witnesses cruelly and unmercifully with bamboo staves and torturing them to death because they would not confess to a crime they did not commit or would not give the evidence the magistrate wanted them to give. In disciplinary theory this grotesque caricature of a Western judge presiding over criminal sittings in China disappears like an optical illusion (which indeed it is), and its place is taken by the much more realistic figure of the imperial district surrogate for the enforcement of discipline, or, more succinctly, the district imperial whip.

The district imperial whip is to be understood as a staff officer of the imperial high command charged in his orderly capacity (he had other capacities) with the duty of maintaining harmony, discipline, and morale among the lower ranks of society within the limits of his local command area, according to the directions of his superiors, so as to maintain the stability of that society and the unchallengeable authority of the existing regime over it. His function was to inculcate, and at all times to insist upon, the dutiful and complete submission and obedience of inferiors toward superiors, whether of the lower ranks toward himself and the gentry, of sons toward fathers, of villagers toward their village heads, of guild members toward their guild leaders, or of any other group members toward their group leader. His duty was to smother dissent and dissension at the source and to teach citizens and group leaders that if dissension arose it must be settled amicably within and by the group wherein it arose. To drive home this message he made it very painful for any persons who failed to settle their quarrels between themselves and came to him to settle their quarrels for them.

The district imperial whip was very sensitive to any appearance of insubordination or disobedience or any deviance from that attitudinal ideal characterized in the family context as *xiao*. He was expected to go to any lengths to suppress it, to compel the resubmission of the offender to hierarchical authority, and to restore the status quo. No duty was more important than this. In Chinese thought the security, and indeed the very survival of society itself, depended upon the dutiful submission of inferiors to status superiors. This cardinal principle was insisted upon and made very explicit for all to see in the attitudes and procedures of physical abasement, such as the koutou (kowtow), that inferiors were compelled to adopt in the presence of their superiors on formal occasions of communication between them. Disciplinary officers were expected, therefore, to use freely the means that were expressly put into their hands for the purpose of compelling this submission, that is, beating and torture.[1] If the subject died, that was unfortunate, but at least a very real threat to the survival of the group, defiance of authority, had been stamped out like a dangerous fire.

The necessity for this resubordination to hierarchical authority of an offender is the rationale behind the requirement that disciplinary officers must always obtain from an offender something called in English, rather misleadingly, a "confession" before proceeding to punishment. The true nature and purpose of this confession is apparent in the term used for it in the Qin and Han periods—the formative years of the Imperial Chinese disciplinary administrative system. The term was *fu,* 服 "submission," meaning a formal act of hierarchical subordination, and not merely, as in the English confession, an evidentiary confirmation of the truth of a set of facts.[2]

This practice of insisting upon a "confession" and using torture as a matter of routine to get it has gravely embarrassed many writers seeking to explain and to justify the Chinese system in terms of Western concepts of criminal administration and has been the occasion for much special pleading.[3] It may be said however that no convincing or satisfactory explanation of the practice has ever been, or can be, offered in terms of Western adjudicative ideals, but that the problem disappears if we look at it in terms of disciplinary theory. In disciplinary theory the main object of the whole procedure is to obtain this submission by any means that are available or can be devised.

In his investigations the district imperial whip was expected to inform himself, as best he could, by his own secret inquiries or those of his spies, what the truth was and who was responsible, and especially he had to be careful not to move against his own status superiors nor any powerful or influential families in his district. When he was satisfied that he had identified someone appropriate for punishment, he had the apparent wrongdoer seized and brought before him in a public castigation ceremony, where the prisoner was expected to acknowledge, kneeling and in chains, the correctness of whatever authority in its wisdom saw fit to do or to say. It was important, but not absolutely essential, that the whip should go to some trouble to get the true offender if he could, and if he had the time; to do so was good for district morale and for personal prestige. But the whip knew that he himself would be in dereliction of duty and in danger of punishment if, after a serious disorder, he was not able to report within a specified time that he had identified and punished those who caused it.

Punishments were the subject of very detailed and complex staff administrative instructions or "Standing Orders for Discipline,"[4] and these had to be followed strictly if the whip himself was to escape the imputation of disobedience to orders. Thus punishment often became the occasion for very bothersome correspondence with superior officers, unless the whip had taken the precaution (which he did whenever he could) of getting his superiors to tell him what punishment to inflict before he pronounced it.

In this connection the researches of Wejen Chang into the files of the Imperial Grand Secretariat Archive held by the Academia Sinica at Taipei are of great interest. The results of Chang's patient study of thousands of these documents undoubtedly constitute a major contribution to the history of Qing jural processes. Chang writes in the idiom of Western jurisprudence, but his results tend strongly to support the view suggested in this book of the Chinese system as a disciplinary one. He finds, for example, that there was constant communication between lower officials and their superiors "at every step, starting immediately after the outbreak of a crime." The superiors' instructions were sent down "with amazing frequency." In some serious cases memorials from the governor-general and even lower officials began to come up to the emperor long before any decision was to be made, reporting facts and seeking instructions. Imperial responses were quickly sent down giving detailed orders. Quite often the decision recommended by lower officials had actually been made by the emperor himself in one of his previous instructions to them.[5] Such a picture is quite repugnant to the existence of any adjudicative system, but is precisely apt to describe a disciplinary staff at work under their commander.

The whip was of course required to report regularly, as in all disciplinary systems, to his superior officers on his actions in the discharge of his duties, and sometimes his superior officers, if what he had done did not please them or suit their policies, would correct him and order him to do something else.

This routine process of the oversight and correction by superior officers of what their subordinates had done has sometimes been confused in the minds of Western writers with appeal procedures in Western legal systems, but the two are quite different in concept, meaning, and purpose and are in no way related.

Another result of the application of disciplinary theory to the Chinese system is that it no longer appears as some strange and complex phenomenon sui generis leaving the legal comparatist in doubt as to what it should be compared with and how to compare it with anything. The system appears now simply as one particular example of a very common type of order control—the disciplinary type—which has long been known in a variety of allied forms all over the world. Indeed it is so much older and so much more widespread than the legal type that it may be taken as characterizing the "common human pattern."[6] The Western legal system and not the Chinese disciplinary one is seen now as the odd one, as a divergent and peculiar style requiring explanation, and calling for reconciliation with the common pattern.

CHAPTER 4

The Mixed Court Prior to 1911

The Mixed Court of the International Settlement at Shanghai was not created pursuant to any treaty or international agreement.[1] It began simply as a branch office of the Shanghai magistracy, located within settlement limits, for the more expeditious disposal of police charges arising locally against Chinese nationals residing in the settlement. The treaties concluded between China and the Western powers following the Opium Wars of the mid-nineteenth century required that charges and complaints against Chinese citizens should be heard and determined in Chinese tribunals. To meet this requirement and for convenience, the Daotai[2] in 1864 at the request of the settlement authorities appointed a Chinese official to reside and to officiate within the settlement for that purpose. He was called "the official north of the Yangjingbang."

Sir Harry Parkes, the British consul-general, provided premises in a Chinese building within the British consulate area where this official might hold his court and insisted that a foreign assessor should sit with him in order to protect foreigners' interests, to check, so far as he could, the grosser abuses inherent in the Chinese system of the administration of order, and to try to develop court procedures more in harmony with Western ideals. It was the court of this official that came to be known, when a consular officer sat with him to monitor the proceedings, as the Mixed Court of the International Settlement, and the "official north of the Yangjingbang" came to be known as the Mixed Court magistrate. After about five months the Daotai agreed that his court should be empowered to hear civil and commercial claims as well as criminal charges.

The arrangements at first were very informal and experimental. In 1869 a set of regulations for the court were drawn up by the Chinese government in Beijing and were promulgated provisionally to be in force for one year, but these regulations were generally disregarded in Shanghai, and no other rules were made until the consuls took the court over in 1911. It should be observed in passing that the circumstances of the creation and constitution of the court in its formative years accord much better with the principles of disciplinary than of legal theory.

The work of the court increased steadily as the population and prosperity of the settlement continued to grow. The presiding Chinese official was allowed gradually to assume enhanced powers of punishment up to a limit of five years imprisonment, amounting in effect to the powers of a *zhixian* or regular district magistrate. He remained nevertheless at all times subordinate to the city magistrate in Shanghai.

By 1911 the work had grown so as to require the services of one senior and two assistant magistrates. At that time the court was sitting six days a week, from 9:15 a.m. for criminal cases, from 2:30 p.m. for mixed civil cases, and from 6:00 p.m. for Chinese civil cases, that is, cases where both parties were Chinese, no foreign interests being involved. Chinese civil cases sometimes lasted into the early hours of the next morning. A foreign assessor always sat with the magistrate, except at hearings of purely Chinese civil cases.

In the criminal jurisdiction of the court the practice developed that no appeals were allowed, but a retrial might be granted if sufficient cause were shown, as for example if material new facts had come to light since the hearing.

On the civil side an appeal was allowed to the Daotai in purely Chinese cases. In cases involving a foreign interest, appeals went to the Daotai and the appropriate foreign consul sitting together as a joint tribunal or mixed court of appeal.

The principles upon which the court arrived at its decisions and the rules of conduct it enforced did not amount to any consistent or coherent system of jurisprudence. In theory it was a Chinese court administering the Chinese system of social order. But the Chinese system was archaic and deficient. Shanghai was, above all, a community of traders, and the Chinese system offered neither a civil nor a commercial code to guide the court in trade disputes. Shanghai was a cosmopolitan city, the home of every kind of vice, perversion, fraud, and crime, but there was no criminal code until 1912. The only extensive and general code of conduct-requirements in China was the *Da Qing Lu Li*. This was a compendium of instructions directed to the officials of the imperial bureaucracy for the administration of the affairs of the empire. It contained in minute detail exact instructions as to the precise type and degree of punishment that disciplinary officers must award in a wide variety of circumstances for deviant behavior offending Chinese ideals of social order. In many respects however these provisions and punishments were not acceptable to the assessors for enforcement in the society of the Western trading enclaves. The Chinese system of criminal administration, while on paper not devoid of ideals admirable in the Western view, was in practice open to the grossest excesses of cruelty and brutality and the gravest abuses of authority for personal gain. It condoned, as a matter of course, the regular flogging and torture of witnesses and accused to get evidence and confessions. It countenanced preferential treatment for persons of rank or wealth. The assessors were simply not prepared to implement the Chinese system as they found it and continually insisted upon departures from it to conform to their own concepts of propriety and their own scales of values.

Any picture of the Mixed Court over any period of its history must be seen against a background of the eternal conflict between the settlement authorities—the municipal council and the consuls—on the one hand, and the Chinese hierarchy of authorities outside the settlement on the other.[3] The foreigners within the settlement were determined at all cost to continue to govern their little trading enclave themselves, in their own way, and to keep out of the settlement the least encroachment of Chinese administrative authority which might bring with it those abuses of "squeeze," arbitrary taxation, and ruthless extortion on pain of torture and death which seemed inseparable from Chinese administration. The foreigners knew that the prosperity, the growth, and the success of the settlement depended very largely on the security it offered from such practices. So strongly did the foreigners feel about this that in 1911 the British consul-general threatened to use military force and to have Shanghai occupied by treaty-power troops if necessary in order to maintain unimpaired the freedom of the International Settlement from the intrusion of Chinese administrative authority.[4]

The Chinese, however, for their part, were determined to find ways of using their magistrate installed in the heart of the forbidden territory to get access to the rich plunder that lay so temptingly before them in the wealth of the affluent Chinese merchants within. As disciplinary theory would lead us to expect, there was no such principle recognized in Imperial China as the independence of the judiciary. The magistrate was an administrative officer bound to obey instructions and could be told whom to arrest and what to do with them when they came before the court.

In the resultant maneuvering for advantage over a period of nearly fifty years from 1864 to 1911, the assessors found themselves committed to a ceaseless struggle not only to restrain the Chinese magistrate but to dominate him in his own court and to bring him around to accept and apply Western procedures and concepts in his administration of order and dispute resolution.

There were, in fact, three procedural features in which the assessors were able to persuade the Chinese magistrates to adopt Western ways, although not in the hearing of Chinese civil cases where the magistrate sat alone. These were, firstly, that counsel were allowed to appear to represent the parties and put argument, a procedure not permitted in traditional Chinese practice. Second, rules of evidence were brought more into line with Western concepts. Issues of fact came to be decided rather more upon firsthand evidence given freely in court than, as previously often happened, upon hearsay, evidence extracted by force, and the magistrate's own investigations and intuitions.[5] Third, torture of parties and witnesses as a regular means of obtaining evidence and confessions fell into disuse, and eventually, soon after the turn of the century, corporal punishment came to be phased out.

But the consuls and the assessors were powerless to change the basic nature of the court. It remained, as it necessarily had to remain, a Chinese court and an integral part of the Imperial Chinese administrative system. Its magistrate, as an official of the system, was bound to do the bidding of his superior officers, and his court remained in essence an instrument for effecting their will, except insofar as the assessors, the consuls, and the municipal council, in a neverending confrontation, were able to substitute their own will. Before 1911, they were never able to get so far as to correct the scandals of the corruption and "squeeze" that were in evidence at all levels, and still less were they able to convert the procedures of the court from the disciplinary to the adjudicative mode nor even to effect anything in the nature of a fusion or an amalgam of the Western and the Chinese systems of dispute resolution and the maintenance of order.

CHAPTER 5

The Mixed Court 1911–27: Historical Dimensions

The revolution of 1911 was, at least on the surface, a very quiet affair at Shanghai. On 3 November the white flag of the rebel cause was raised and a mixed group of republican military forces took possession of the city almost without opposition, and by 4 November the revolution, for Shanghai, was over. The Manzhou dynasty had fallen and with its fall the imperial system of government that had served China for more than two thousand years was gone forever from Shanghai.[1]

The Mixed Court, being an agency of the Manzhou regime, also fell a casualty to the revolution. The affairs of the court at this stage were, in the eyes of the consular body and the European community, in a scandalous state and in need of urgent reform.

Corruption was prevalent at all levels from the senior magistrate down to the lowest runner and hanger-on. The court buildings were dirty and dilapidated and the courtrooms black with dirt and grime. The detention house and the female prison were in a state of indescribable filth and in wretched repair, although only three years old. There were no proper cooking or sanitary arrangements and the cells and corridors were strewn with refuse. The prisons were infested with rats and were a hotbed of disease. Small children were living there with parents who were undergoing long terms of imprisonment. Extortion was unchecked. Gambling and opium-smoking among warders and prisoners was rife. But the court was under Chinese authority, and the consuls and the municipal council were not empowered to intervene nor to check the abuses.[2]

Now, however, when republican forces were taking possession of the city, it was time for Manzhou officials to quit. Senior Magistrate Bao, a Manzhou, and his assistant magistrate Teh, also Manzhou, disappeared, escaping perhaps by boat down the river. When they had gone it was found that they had been guilty of extensive embezzlement of Mixed Court funds. Audit disclosed a deficiency in the court accounts of sixty thousand taels.[3] The most junior assistant magistrate, Wang Jiaxi, and the magistrate of the French Mixed Court, Nie Zongxi, both Chinese, remained at their posts.

Meanwhile the consular body nominated Guan Jiongzhi, a Chinese official who had some years previously occupied the post of assistant magistrate on the Mixed Court, to be chief magistrate in place of the runaway Bao, and the Daotai, in one of the last official acts permitted him by the consuls, duly appointed Guan chief magistrate accordingly. But as such Guan was an appointee of the Imperial Manzhou Government. Would the Chinese within the settlement accept him, and would the republican authorities execute his warrants and recognize his process outside the settlement?

The consuls were in a difficult position. The only government the treaty powers allowed them to recognize was the Imperial Manzhou Government, still surviving at Beijing. But that government had lost all authority in Shanghai. So far as the International Settlement was concerned there was a power vacuum in provincial government. How was the Mixed Court to be continued and under whose auspices? Who would appoint and pay the magistrates in future? A Mixed Court magistrate appointed and paid by the revolutionaries, and subservient to their direction in the Chinese tradition, would go far toward delivering up the wealth of the International Settlement, or at least the very large Chinese component of it, into the hands of the republican government and would spell the end of the prosperity and usefulness of Shanghai as one of the great international ports of the world.

The British consul-general, Everard Fraser, realized how necessary it was to forestall any move by the republicans to gain a foothold in the administration of the settlement by appointing their own political activists to be magistrates of the Mixed Court. He saw also that the consuls might take advantage of this opportunity to reform and rehabilitate the court and the prisons and to ensure tighter restraints in future against peculation and corruption on the part of the magistrates. Accordingly he drafted a proclamation by which the consular body would step in and confirm the existing magistrates, Guan Jiongzhi, Wang Jiaxi, and Nie Zongxi in the occupancy of their official positions, and from which it would become clear that the consuls were now assuming responsibility for the control and management of the affairs of the Mixed Court, its magistrates, and its prisons, and he submitted this proclamation to the consular body.

At the same time he let it be known to the rebel leaders at Shanghai, with his minister's approval, that any attempt to modify the special status of the settlement or its autonomous administration by the consular body and by the municipal council, would be met with the occupation of Shanghai by the military forces of the treaty powers.

Faced with this prospect, and not yet strong enough to risk a direct confrontation with the treaty powers, the revolutionaries bowed to the inevitable. Wu Tingfang and Wen Tsung-yao, commissioner and deputy commissioner for foreign affairs in the republican government, called on Consul-general Fraser and agreed to let the existing magistrates carry on if the consular body was satisfied with them.

Fraser now prevailed upon the consular body to step into the power vacuum and act. After hesitation on the part of some of the consuls, and after some minor amendments, his proclamation was agreed to. It was accepted, signed by eighteen consuls on behalf of the eighteen treaty powers, translated into Chinese, and posted up at the doors of the Mixed Court on 11 November.[4] On 14 November the municipal police marched in, took physical possession of the court and jail premises and the books and records, dismissed the court runners, ejected the opium peddlers, the visitors and relatives of the prisoners, and all the hangers-on, and mounted guard.[5]

Having taken the plunge, the consular body proceeded to introduce a number of reforms in further arbitrary arrogation to itself of group-disciplinary authority.[6] It began by greatly extending the jurisdiction and powers of the Mixed Court magistrates in criminal cases. It instructed the court by a simple letter that the previous practice of sending to the city magistrates for hearing and decision all cases that seemed serious enough to call for a penalty of more than five years imprisonment would cease, and that the Mixed Court itself would, in the future, hear and determine every charge brought before it, whatever the gravity of the offense, up to and including capital charges.[7]

The consular body then proceeded to fix the amount of the salaries and allowances to be paid to the magistrates and directed that they be defrayed out of certain Chinese government assets in the hands of the senior consul.

Early in December the consular body vested responsibility for the financial affairs of the court and for the day-to-day administration of the court's business in the municipal council, acting through a registrar.

Finally the consuls determined upon and effected a significant change in the constitution of the court when sitting for the hearing of purely Chinese civil cases. Up to this time such cases had always been heard and disposed of by the Chinese magistrate sitting alone, and counsel were not permitted to appear.

The consuls now proposed that in future in these cases, an assessor of one of the treaty powers would sit with the Chinese magistrate, the appearance of counsel would be permitted, and the judgment of the court would not be valid unless signed by both the Chinese magistrate and the foreign assessor.[8] But the consuls trod warily. They were about to challenge very powerful and deeply entrenched vested interests. In the group-disciplinary organization of Chinese merchant communities, settlement of trade disputes, administration of bankruptcies, the winding up of partnerships, and all such commercial causes were primarily the responsibility, not of the state, but of the group. The function of state power as represented by the magistrate was primarily to uphold the authority of the group leaders and support their decisions, rather than to investigate the merits of a dispute and give an independent judgment. In Shanghai this meant that decisive authority in dispute resolution and the government of differences in commercial matters between purely Chinese interests lay with the Chinese Chamber of Commerce and the guilds. If a magistrate were brought into a dispute at all, then the influence of the chamber and the guilds on his judgment was likely to be determinative. This was a prerogative and a source of power of which the chamber and the guilds were very jealous, and the consuls were seeking to take it from them.

A meeting was accordingly arranged for an exchange of views between the foreign assessors, representing the consuls, and representatives of the chamber of commerce, the Chinese banks, the guilds, and the Chinese merchant community. Matters were discussed at length and it became clear that the consuls were resolute in their determination to have their way, and that the Chinese merchants were not prepared, at this stage, to fight the issue, at least not openly.[9] Accordingly the reform was put in force, the consular body issued a set of *Rules of Procedure in Chinese Civil Cases*, and from 8 January 1912, in pursuance of those rules, a foreign assessor sat with the Chinese magistrate in all Chinese civil cases, and the court was compelled to hear counsel for the parties.[10] As a result, the power of merchant group leaders to control the magistrates in dispute resolution in the settlement was substantially curtailed, and it was about fourteen years before signs of effective merchant interference began to reappear.

The republican leaders were far too busy with the ongoing revolution to concern themselves very much with what the consuls were doing to the Mixed Court. Wu Tingfang, as minister for foreign affairs, addressed a series of directives to military governors in which he said, among other things:

In Shanghai some provisional arrangements have been rendered an unjust necessity by the importance and magnitude of foreign interests. . . . Recovery of authority at Shanghai where civil and police administration is in the hands of foreigners must be left until the political situation is securely established. . . . The officials hitherto appointed by the Manzhou dynasty to the Mixed Court at Shanghai were for the most part a degenerate lot who fostered rank corruption, and when the City seceded to the Republican cause the foreign powers actually arrogated to themselves the Court's functions and have not yet handed them back to national control. This sort of proceeding naturally calls for challenge, and some scheme by which the Court's authority can be wrested back is vitally imperative. Meantime civil and military Republican authority must not interfere.[11]

But despite the simmering resentment of the Chinese disclosed in this proclamation, the consuls stood firm. After their reforms the effective power of appointment to the Mixed Court remained at all times with the consular body, and no appointee was ever in doubt that he owed his appointment to that body and that it was the consuls he must satisfy if he were to keep it.

During the life of the Mixed Court under consular control from 11 November 1911 to 31 December 1926, two assistant magistrates, Wang Jiaxi and Wang Douji, died in office; one assistant magistrate, Tsang, resigned; one parttime assistant magistrate, Nie Zongxi, who was also magistrate of the French Mixed Court, was withdrawn from the International Mixed Court for fulltime service at the French court; and additional assistant magistrates were appointed from time to time as the work load increased, until the total complement of the Mixed Court in 1926 comprised the senior magistrate and six assistant magistrates. Guan Jiongzhi, the senior magistrate, retained his position for the whole period. He was a remarkable man, and the success of the court in its Chinese dimension was undoubtedly due in no small measure to his strength of character and to his work in the senior role.

For the rest of the life of the Mixed Court, the supervision of its affairs by the assessors, the registrar, and the auditors was much too tight to leave room for the rise of any systematic practice of subornation of the magistrates or any such notorious scandal as that of the Manzhou magistrates who absconded with the funds.

But despite this, judicial subversion did not entirely disappear. The focus of corruption, however, shifted from the magistrates to the consuls—or at least to some of the consuls of some of the lesser treaty powers. There developed a practice by which an unscrupulous consul of a treaty power could grant a Chinese citizen the protection of consular recognition as a citizen of that treaty power. This gave him the benefit of extraterritoriality. No action, whether civil or criminal, could then be taken against him in the Mixed Court. He could only be attacked in the consular court of the power protecting him. Since the consul himself comprised that court and was the final authority in Shanghai on any question arising in that court, it was not difficult for him to find a reason to dismiss the case against his protégé. If the protected Chinese desired to sue another Chinese he did so in the Mixed Court, whereupon his protecting consul claimed an interest in the case on the ground that one of his "nationals" was a party. This entitled him to sit as assessor at the hearing and this generally meant that he was able to ensure a decision in his protégé's favor.

The British and American assessors did their best to bring these abuses under control. It was impossible however to escape the simple fact that the only authority competent, in the final analysis, to say whether a particular individual was or was not a citizen of a particular sovereign power was that power itself, through its proper instrumentalities and officials, namely, in Shanghai at that time, its consul. As a result protected persons could, and did, simply ignore the court's process. The only avenue of relief open to an aggrieved party was to petition the consul's superior, the minister for the power concerned, in Beijing, and ask him to direct his consul in Shanghai to withdraw consular protection.

However these abuses were never such as to inhibit the steady growth of the court's business. Their principal relevance may be seen in the ammunition they provided for activists to use in attacking on emotional and nationalistic lines the institution of extraterritoriality, with a view to its abolition.

The British and American zeal for reform of the Mixed Court was not limited to the moral and ideological dimensions of the court's activities and functions but extended to the physical and material setting as well. Within a few months of the assumption of management by the muncipal council the court buildings had been cleaned, repaired, renovated, painted, improved, and extended to provide airy, well-lit, well-ventilated courtrooms, with convenient chambers and offices for the magistrates, assessors, registrar, and court officials. The house of detention, flanking the court on one side, and the women's prison, flanking it on the other, were reconditioned, cleaned, and painted; wooden floors were taken up and concrete floors laid, rat infestation eliminated, and proper dormitories, cooking facilities, bathrooms, laundries, sanitation arrangements, and drainage installed. The young children living in degradation, misery, suffering, and neglect with their imprisoned mothers were removed (except for nursing babies up to about four or five months old) for their proper care to a charitable institution supported by the municipal council.[12]

In May 1916 further alterations, extensions, and modernizations of the court facilities took place. The main courtroom itself was converted to resemble the average British police court with a dock for prisoners, tables and chairs for counsel and parties, and seats for the public. An additional courtroom was provided to cope with the greatly increased work.[13] An observer writing in 1916 reported that

> Short terms in gaol are rather welcomed than otherwise by many of the men, for they mean to them shelter, good food, warm blankets, and a chance to learn a trade under the most favourable conditions. Indeed it has come to pass that many habitual offenders are in the habit of flocking to Shanghai as soon as the cold weather sets in with the express purpose of putting up at the gaol for the winter.[14]

During the fifteen years 1911 to 1926, the trade of Shanghai and the population of the International Settlement increased significantly and the work of the Mixed Court increased accordingly. The population grew from 13,536 foreigners and 488,005 Chinese—a total of 501,541 according to the census of 1910—to 29,947 foreigners and 810,279 Chinese—a total of 840,226 according to the census of 1925. The total maritime customs revenue of the Port of Shanghai (an index of the trade of Shanghai) was, in 1911, 11,786,662 Haikwan taels and in 1926, 33,630,877 Haikwan taels.[15] The cases dealt with by the Mixed Court increased, in its criminal division, from 46,050 criminal charges in 1912 to 103,932 charges in 1926; in its foreign civil division from 86 hearings in 1913 to 606 hearings in 1926; and in its Chinese civil division from 1592 hearings in 1915 to 2848 hearings in 1926.[16] In addition, in 1926, 1209 rent cases were heard and 206 inquests were held. This amounted to a very heavy workload for the magistrates and the assessors. For instance, in 1924 the court entered convictions in 90,331 cases and dismissals in 1223 cases in its criminal division, and it concluded 1145 Chinese civil cases and 655 foreign civil cases—a total of 93,354 cases disposed of in the year. Allowing for the circumstance that 68,791 of the criminal convictions were bail forfeitures not requiring a hearing, there still remained a total of 24,563 hearings in that year.[17] Divided among five magistrates this meant very nearly 5,000 cases heard and determined by each magistrate in addition to his share of inquests and ejectments. The magistrates and assessors were seriously overworked, and in that year the number of magistrates was raised to seven and two additional regular assessors appointed.[18] Escarra wrote of the Mixed Court in 1926, "C'est peut-être le tribunal le plus important du monde par le nombre des affaires" (It is perhaps the most important law court in the world, according to the number of cases it hears).[19] It is significant that when the Jiangsu Provisional Court took the place of the Mixed Court in January 1927 and took over the work being done by its seven magistrates, it started with a team of eleven judges on the bench and the appointment of two more awaited.[20] Dr. John C. H. Wu, who was one of those eleven judges, has written that "every morning there were brought to me hundreds of cases of minor infractions of traffic regulations each to be fined not more than a dollar," and that the system worked in respect to those cases, like a "judicial slot machine."[21]

The Mixed Court accepted petitions for relief in every kind of claim, whether originating in law or in equity or in group discipline or merely in someone's sense of injury or need.[22] It assumed competence, without limit in respect of amount in dispute in legal proceedings of every kind, including personal actions, actions involving title to land, distraint for rent, ejectment, forfeiture of leases, partnership accounts and winding-up, bankruptcy, probate, admiralty, and divorce, and some miscellaneous proceedings such as the petition for record. This was a noncontentious proceeding where the registrar simply accepted and took into the court files some document or other for permanent record—perhaps a power of attorney, or a family settlement, or the rules of a guild, or the objects of a charity, or something of which an accessible, authentic, and unalterable record was sought to be made.

Punishments imposed for criminal offenses were fines, imprisonment, and the death penalty—sanctions familiar to Western legal practice—and expulsion from the settlement—a concept familiar to group-disciplinary practice.

In view of the consuls' instructions to the court when they seized control of it that the previous practice of sending serious cases to the city magistrate for disposal would cease and the Mixed Court itself would in future hear and dispose of all cases of whatever gravity, there could now be no limit to the severity of the sentence the court might be called upon to impose. The assessors had no scruples about imposing sentences of ten and twenty years or life imprisonment, but the Chinese magistrates were not prepared to arrogate to themselves powers of punishment beyond the limit of five years imprisonment for which they had the authority of the Chinese government under the old system. This might have provided a serious impediment, but the magistrates were able to get around the difficulty, satisfying both their own consciences and the consuls' requirements, by entering as their judgment in such cases "five years imprisonment, after which the prisoner will again be brought before the court," and at his next appearance the prisoner would be awarded a further five years, and so on.[23]

Prison sentences were enforced in municipal jails within settlement limits and without reference to any Chinese authority, but the death penalty was treated differently. The consuls and the municipal council refrained from carrying out on their own responsibility the execution of prisoners within the settlement. The practice was to hand over all prisoners meriting the death penalty to competent Chinese authorities outside the settlement for execution. Sometimes the sentence might be announced by the assessor and entered boldly on his record sheet in English, as "sentenced to death," followed by a direction that the prisoner be handed over to Chinese authorities for execution.

The Chinese magistrate, for his part, was careful never to exceed in his endorsement the limited authority which the Mixed Court magistrate had possessed before the consuls took charge. He simply did in these cases what the Mixed Court magistrate had always done in serious cases—declared the nature of the offense and ordered that the matter be passed on to superior authority for such action as might be deemed appropriate.[24]

But the effect of a capital judgment pronounced by the Mixed Court, however it may have been expressed in the court records, was always the same. It meant that the prisoner was to be delivered out of the custody and control of the Mixed Court and the settlement authorities into the hands of Chinese authorities outside the settlement accompanied by a copy of the Mixed Court proceedings and a recommendation that he be executed. The Chinese were then in a position to deal with such a prisoner in any way they saw fit.

Sometimes they would refuse to carry out an execution and would return the prisoner to the custody of the Mixed Court. The court would thereupon commute the sentence to a term of imprisonment.[25]

Sometimes the Chinese would neither execute the prisoner nor return him, but award him a mild punishment which would mean that in a short time he would be free again.

If however the assessors and the municipal police ensured that the prisoner was delivered into the hands of the military authorities at the arsenal and not to the commissioner for foreign affairs and the city magistrate in Shanghai, this procedure regularly meant that after a short inquiry or review of the case the military commander would promptly execute the condemned man.

Sometimes the military commander would execute criminals merely on the finding of the Mixed Court without any further inquiry. In the aftermath of the riots and boycott of mid-1925 an official of the China Association reported in September:

> This afternoon I saw General Hsing Shih-lien at Lunghua [the arsenal]. . . . As to the handing over by the [Shanghai Municipal] Council of the sentenced prisoners for execution he confirmed the arrangement I had already made with Colonel Chin, his second in command, namely that he would receive them in batches of about twenty weekly and would shoot them on the Mixed Court records without re-trial. The first batch was sent over on Monday and will be disposed of within the next few days. He will parade them as publicly as possible in each case before the event and will exhibit some of their heads in baskets at suitable places afterwards.[26]

By Article 40 of the Provisional Criminal Code of China it was provided that "sentence of death shall not be executed unless confirmed by the Ministry of Justice," and by Article 38 that "sentence of death shall be executed by strangulation within the precincts of the prison." These restrictions in the criminal code, however, did not count for much in Shanghai during the warlord period, when distant provincial governments paid only such attention to the central government in Beijing as suited their purposes. In particular, military commanders and military courts were free to do very much as they pleased irrespective of any legal restraints. The International Commission on Extraterritoriality reported in 1926 that, "by virtue of Chinese law itself the legal position of the military renders them immune from the jurisdiction of the ordinary courts, while their power, in fact, often renders them immune from all courts."[27] Hence the settlement authorities found it advantageous to hand over condemned men to the military commander at the arsenal rather than to the civil power in the city. Execution took place by shooting and was generally carried out on the execution grounds at the arsenal.

The Mixed Court did not hesitate to apply the death penalty in cases that seemed to call for it. In 1924 ninety-six executions took place at the instance of the Mixed Court.[28] In 1923, in rendering up a pregnant woman for execution, the court asked that she be given the benefit of the Chinese custom and practice in such cases, namely that the execution be delayed until the expiration of one hundred days after delivery.[29]

Very relevant to any study of the Mixed Court and the part played by it in the introduction of the ideas of Western jurisprudence into Chinese thought is a consideration of the body of lawyers who practiced before the court. Apart from the independence of the judiciary, one of the most obvious and significant of the differences between Western legal systems and Far Eastern disciplinary systems of dispute resolution and the maintenance of order in society is the presence in the West of a strong and independent bar of professional advocates and the absence of any such thing, or even of the concept, in the Chinese system. Mixed Court practice enabled Chinese lawyers not only to study at first hand this key institution on Chinese soil, but also to participate in the operation of the legal process themselves as members of such a bar.

There were on the court roll of those admitted to practice in 1917 seventy-four practitioners with foreign qualifications, of whom thirty-five were British, fourteen American, six Chinese, five Japanese, two French, and the remainder German, Austrian, Portuguese, Italian, and Spanish.[30] There were also on the rolls about five locally qualified Chinese. In mid-1926 there were "about 100 foreign attorneys practising before the Mixed Court."[31] In addition to their work before the Mixed Court these lawyers practiced before one or more of the many other courts and tribunals sitting in Shanghai, particularly before their own national and consular courts. There was, as well, a considerable volume of conveyancing and other noncontentious work available to the law firms.

Law practice in Shanghai was not easy. In the experience of Norwood F. Allman, an American practitioner, the lawyer

> might be in the Chinese court one day, the British the next, the French or American Court another. . . . A fluency in French, plus a good working knowledge of the Code Napoleon and of Chinese and English law was highly desirable. It was taken for granted that the American lawyer in Shanghai knew something about international law, maritime law, the laws of the District of Columbia, the decisions of the Federal courts, equity, and the laws of most of the forty-eight of these United States. Cases in the American court frequently turned upon the law of any one of the States not to mention the laws of the Philippine Islands.[32]

The Mixed Court never attempted to regulate, as Western courts do, the professional charges made by practitioners for their services. There was no prescribed scale of lawyers' fees and no system of taxation of costs. This was chiefly because foreign lawyers, the subjects of extraterritorial powers, were not amenable to the court's jurisdiction and the court had no means of enforcing any scale of costs or any order it might make against such practitioners. The general rule was that, successful or unsuccessful, the litigant had to pay his own costs.

Legal practice in Shanghai could be lucrative for able lawyers. Dr. John C. H. Wu has written that when he started private practice in Shanghai in 1930 (which was after the Mixed Court had been abolished and its place taken by a purely Chinese court):

> within the very first month I received so many retainerships and cases that my income amounted to no less than forty thousand taels—almost equivalent to forty thousand American dollars. I had earned in one month more than all the salaries I had got as a judge and as a professor put together.[33]

Sir John Pratt, in one of his somewhat bitter criticisms of the Mixed Court, commented that

> Chinese involved in civil or criminal cases believed that their chances of success depended upon securing the intervention of a foreign consul or the services of a foreign lawyer. The foreign lawyers, of whom there were far too many in Shanghai and of whom far too many were not honest, reaped a golden harvest.[34]

But the days of the "golden harvest" for the foreign lawyers were numbered. On 31 December 1926 the Mixed Court went out of existence and its place was taken by the Jiangsu Provisional Court. Before that court foreigners were not permitted to appear except when a foreigner or the Shanghai Municipal Council was a party to the proceedings.

Control over the constitution and jurisdiction of the Mixed Court had been assumed and justified by the consular body in the first place only as a temporary measure to meet an emergency. The state of emergency passed once the republican government had become firmly established and had been recognized by the treaty powers. The United States granted recognition on 2 May 1913 and all the other treaty powers on or before 7 October 1913. Thereafter the return to the Chinese government of disciplinary authority over its own nationals within the settlement was inevitable and became only a question of how and when.

But the diplomatic body desired first to ensure, if it could, that the reforms carried out while the court was under consular control would be preserved. In particular the diplomatic body wanted to ensure that the court would not become a mere administrative instrumentality obedient to the direction of superior authority. If this were allowed to happen then any government for the time being could attack with disciplinary sanctions and compulsions political refugees and wealthy merchants sheltering in the political neutrality of the settlement. The diplomatic body also sought to use the return of the Mixed Court as a bargaining counter with which to ensure an extension of the geographical limits of the International Settlement. But this the Chinese Ministry of Foreign Affairs would not allow.

In 1915 agreement for rendition seemed assured on all points except the extension of settlement limits, a concession which remained unacceptable to the Chinese. Thereafter spasmodic indecisive negotiations dragged on for years without much apparent enthusiasm by either side for an early conclusion, and in fact no conclusion was ever reached at a national level. In the meantime central government in Beijing deteriorated and control of the people and the territory of China became fragmented among the warlords. As early as 1924 Sir John Jordan had written:

> I wish we could get to bedrock and admit that there is no government in China in the ordinary sense of the word, but I suppose we must keep up the fiction of holding Peking responsible for the disintegrated mass of warring *tuchuns* who now run the country.[35]

On 29 November 1926 in Beijing the "Regency Cabinet" resigned for lack of funds to carry on the government, and there was then "no Government in China north of the Yangtze."[36] There was no longer any sovereign authority in China even in name to whom rendition might have been made, or by whom jurisdiction might have been assumed and exercised over the Chinese in the settlement. The Foreign Office in London recorded the situation as follows:

> At the present moment His Majesty's Government recognize no government in China as the Government of China. The Government formerly recognized has ceased to exist. They recognize that there is a State called China which has its capital in Peking and they maintain a diplomatic mission there, but there is no person residing at Peking whom they recognize as the Head of the Chinese State nor any government which they recognize as the Government of China.[37]

The warlords had put China's sovereignty into total eclipse.

It is instructive and important here to notice the ambivalence of Chinese attitudes toward sovereignty and extraterritoriality. The words of Chinese advocates in the international forum protested the inviolability of Chinese sovereignty and the iniquity of the affronts offered to it by extraterritoriality. The actions of Chinese leaders on their home ground demonstrated a cynical contempt for Chinese sovereignty and a callous indifference to extraterritoriality. It was China's own citizens, the warlords, who offered China's sovereignty the ultimate humiliation far beyond the encroachments of the foreign powers—they put China's sovereignty into complete abeyance and suspended its credibility in the councils of the nations. A United States Department of State memorandum on "Surrender of Extraterritorial Jurisdiction in China" records that

> A candid Chinese once admitted that the danger to China was not extraterritorial foreigners but extraterritorial Chinese. He referred of course to the hordes of military officers and their satellites and soldiers over whom no civil court dreams of asserting jurisdiction as well as to powerful politicians who are equally immune.[38]

The simple explanation is that sovereignty and territoriality are, as we have already noticed, abstract concepts located in the jurisprudence of Western legal systems and had no place in the disciplinary and group-hierarchical organization of Chinese society nor in its thought patterns. Sovereignty was so irrelevant, indeed, that its eclipse accelerated rather than delayed the restitution of control of the Mixed Court to Chinese authority. The Mixed Court was not a child of jurisprudence, nor was it fathered in sovereignty. It was abolished in the same way that it was born—by the mere fiat of local group administrators.

Ever since the 1914–18 European war had made it clear for all to see that the Western powers were not united or invulnerable, political pressures had been building up in China directed to the reassertion by Chinese authorities of command and control over Chinese nationals living in the settlements. These pressures came to a head in the burst of strong antiforeign and anti-Christian agitation that swept across China in 1925 and culminated in widespread demonstrations, strikes, and a boycott of foreign trade. The strikes and the boycott were devastatingly effective. Forced against their will into a gesture of conciliation, the China Association and the British Chamber of Commerce held a joint meeting of members on 31 August 1925 and passed a resolution expressing sympathy with China's national aspirations and supporting in principle Chinese representation on the municipal council and the rendition of the Mixed Court.[39] Sir Austen Chamberlain, the British Foreign Secretary, was prepared to step in at the highest level and surrender consular supervision of the court altogether, if negotiations became deadlocked on that point.[40] Dr. Jacob G. Schurman, the American minister at Peking, had advised the secretary of state in Washington in 1924 that he was in favor of returning the court to Chinese control.[41]

But the weight of all these opinions and political pressures was not sufficient. The consuls, the men on the spot, were the persons immediately responsible for the peace, order, and good government of the settlement, and they were not to be stampeded. In May 1925 the consular body had insisted, in representations to the diplomatic body in Beijing, that foreign assessors must remain in all criminal cases or the preservation of order in the settlement would become impossible.[42] As time passed, moreover, the emergency began to subside and the question of rendition became less urgent. The street riots were quelled, and by the end of September the boycott was broken and trade was returning to normal. Agreement on terms for the rendition of the Mixed Court seemed as remote as ever.

But the Chinese had a weapon that was much more direct and deadly than public opinion and popular agitation, and now they proceeded to use it. The demise of the Mixed Court, when it came, was the result not of political pressures, but of juridical compulsions.

The Achilles heel of the Mixed Court lay in the means of execution of its judgments and process. Within the settlement all was well. The municipal police stood by and gave effect to the court's orders—even to the extent that when the judgment written by the assessor differed from that written by the magistrate, as it sometimes did, the police would act upon the assessors's version rather than the magistrate's.[43] But execution of process outside settlement limits presented difficulties from the beginning. It was dependent on the willing cooperation of officials of purely Chinese instrumentalities, which was not always forthcoming. To get it, the best weapon that the consuls had was to threaten that the cooperation of the settlement police in executing within the settlement the warrants and judgments of Chinese courts and authorities outside the settlement would be withdrawn, and this tactic was usually successful. A sort of uneasy truce was maintained of necessity for the benefit of both parties. But now the Chinese authorities stepped up a campaign of noncooperation, and the consuls found that the threat of reprisals was no longer effective.

In August 1925 the commissioner of foreign affairs returned a warrant of arrest, issued by the Mixed Court and forwarded to him for execution outside the settlement, with a flat refusal to act. The reason given was that, "as the Shanghai Mixed Court is not a legally constituted Judicial Court so they possess no authority whatever to effect any arrest," and consequently there was no obligation on any Chinese official to render any assistance.[44] The senior consul protested and ended his letter by saying,

> if the Chinese authorities persist in this attitude the Consular Body may be compelled to consider the advisability of instructing the competent Settlement authorities to refrain from giving any assistance in the execution of warrants and summonses issued by the Chinese authorities.[45]

But this threat no longer availed. The only result was a letter from the commissioner of foreign affairs reaffirming the Chinese attitude.[46] In other cases of refusal to act upon Mixed Court process the authorities outside the settlement were equally adamant.

The statement that the Shanghai Mixed Court was "not a legally constituted Judicial Court" was based on a judgment of the Supreme Court of China delivered in 1917. The Supreme Court decided in effect that the Mixed Court as constituted since the consuls took control in 1911 had no lawful jurisdiction over Chinese nationals and that consequently its proceedings and decisions were of no legal effect in China.

This judgment will be examined more closely in the next chapter. It is sufficient to note here that since the effect of the judgment was only to deny to the Mixed Court any lawful jurisdiction, the Mixed Court could, and did, simply ignore it. The Mixed Court was operating in the context of a group-disciplinary system of order, not an adjudicative one, and its proceedings were rooted in disciplinary theory, not in jurisprudence. Jurisdiction is a concept of jurisprudence, a question of law, and of no significance in a disciplinary system. In the theory of disciplinary systems, as we have seen, a court's survival is a question of competence, not jurisdiction, and competence is a question of fact not of law.[47] The decision of the Supreme Court meant no more in 1925 than it had done at any time since it was delivered eight years previously, in 1917. Its use now was simply a colorable excuse for the challenge that was being mounted. The difficulties that the Mixed Court was experiencing did not stem from lack of jurisdiction in law, but from lack of competence in fact. The competence of a disciplinary tribunal depends on its ability to enforce its judgments. The Mixed Court now found itself unable to compel enforcement of its judgments by agencies beyond settlement limits. True, the court was not faced with extinction. Its competence within the settlement was not impaired, but its competence outside the settlement was gone. Once the court could no longer bare its teeth outside the settlement its usefulness to the settlement was gone. It was reduced to the status of a "paper tiger"—anybody could escape its bite by simply crossing into the native city.

The consuls had no answer to this challenge. They were in no position in 1925, as they had been in 1911 when they took over the court, to use threats of force if they did not get their way. This time it was the consuls' turn to bow to the inevitable. The tide of Western ambition in China was on the ebb, and no Western nation could be expected at this late hour to deploy its military forces in China outside the settlement to save the Mixed Court. The power that prevailed in the southeastern regions of China outside the settlement was at this time the provincial government of Jiangsu (Kiangsu) under the authority of the Dujun, Sun Chuanfang. Sun's warlord rule extended also over Zhejiang (Chekiang), Anhui (Anhwei), Jiangxi (Kiangsi), and Fujian (Fukien). He had declared these provinces independent of Beijing in December 1925. The cooperation of the officials of this administration was essential if the processes of any court within the settlement were to be made effective outside it.

When, therefore, in late April 1926 Marshal Sun suggested that local negotiations might be opened between the consular body and the provincial government of Jiangsu to resolve the impasse, the consuls at once responded. The British consul-general, Sir Sydney Barton, took the lead and, within little more than two months, terms for the rendition of the court to the provincial government were agreed upon and received the approval of the diplomatic body at Beijing—without prejudice to the arrangements being superseded if at any time an effective central government of China should appear and come to some other agreement with the treaty powers.[48] The provincial government of Jiangsu was not a sovereign power. It was not recognized by His Majesty's Government as a legitimate government, and the consuls had dealt with it merely "as a *de facto* local administration under the authority of Sun Chuanfang."[49] An agreement drafted by Sir Sydney Barton and embodying the terms of the arrangements was signed on 23 September 1926 and rendition was effected on 1 January 1927.[50] By the terms of the agreement, the Mixed Court was not preserved and returned to Chinese control as an entity, but was abolished as from 31 December 1926, and its place was taken by the establishment within the settlement of the Shanghai Provisional Court of Jiangsu manned by legally qualified Chinese judges appointed by the provincial government without reference to the consuls. Consular deputies and consular officials were not permitted to sit with the judges except when foreign interests were involved and in some types of criminal prosecution.[51]

This court at its inception was simply an ad hoc creation of Sun Chuanfang's de facto administration and no more the instrumentality of any sovereign power than the Mixed Court had been. But three years later it was superseded by a district court under central government control and became integrated at last with the Chinese judicial system as a legitimate unit of the hierarchy of modern courts being developed by the Nationalist government.

CHAPTER 6

Mixed Court Administration of Order Analyzed

This chapter will examine the question, What claim did the Mixed Court have after 1911 to legality? That is to say, what claim did it have to exercise a legitimate jurisdiction according to the doctrines of Western jurisprudence over Chinese citizens on Chinese soil? And if the validity of its claim is in doubt, if it is hard to find any sound basis for its exercise of a *jurisdiction* in terms of legal theory and the requirements of a legal system, did it have any claim to *competence* in terms of disciplinary theory and the requirements of a group-disciplinary system?

Second, the question, Upon what principles did the court act in coming to its decisions? will be discussed. Freed of imperial Chinese control and no longer subject to direction from outside the settlement, how far was it able to shed its disciplinary character and adopt the Western mode of independent adjudication against predetermined rules? If it applied rules, where did it get them, and upon what compulsions did it accept them? How far, on the contrary, did the court continue to follow the old system and do whatever it thought best in the interests of the group and in support of the group leaders' policies according to the disciplinary mode?

THE LEGITIMACY OF THE MIXED COURT

It may be said at the outset that the court itself at all times claimed to be a legitimate Chinese court and an integral part of the Chinese judicial system. It boldly assumed and exercised, at the instigation of the consuls, an unlimited authority over Chinese citizens in the settlement, sitting in judgment on them in civil cases and submitting them to punishments in criminal proceedings.

Delivering judgment in the case of *Rosenberg China Company v. Far Eastern Branch of the Russian Volunteer Fleet* in 1924, Joseph E.

Jacobs, assessor, said, "The defendant's counsel . . . inferred that this court is not a Chinese court. It is true that this court occupies an anomalous position in the Chinese judicial system, but it is, nevertheless, regardless of this fact an integral part of the Chinese judicial system."[1]

Furthermore, this claim of the Mixed Court to the status of a legitimate Chinese court within the Chinese system was expressly acknowledged in the United States Court for China. In the case of the *Chinese Maritime Customs v. American-Oriental Banking Corporation, Garnishee,* in 1922, Judge Lobingier said:

> The International Mixed Court at Shanghai is a recognized Chinese tribunal and we take it that its judgments are to be treated here as those of the courts of a sister nation, prima facie valid, and impeachable only upon a clear and decisive showing.[2]

The status of the Mixed Court as a Chinese court was also recognized by the British court in Shanghai, that is, His Britannic Majesty's Supreme Court for China. In an order made in 1914 upon an application by trustees for advice and direction, Mr. Justice Bourne said:

> When, in such cases [as these], this Court is doubtful which of several claimants is by Chinese law entitled to the beneficial interest, our practice has been to refer that question to the appropriate Chinese Court, and to adopt in a proper case its findings. That question in this case has already been determined by the Mixed Court and clearly determined with perfect justice.[3]

It is to be noted that in neither of these two cases was the court's claim to legitimate Chinese status disputed or argued. The question remains, will such a claim bear investigation in terms of Western jurisprudence?

It may be granted that the assumption by the consuls of responsibility for the court in November 1911 was probably justified by the conditions of emergency then prevailing. *Salus populi suprema lex* (the safety of the people is the highest law). Perhaps also the retention by the consuls of control might similarly be excused until the political situation had stabilized, that is to say until the treaty powers had formally recognized the new state of the Republic of China and the government of Yuan Shikai. This they did in October 1913. But thereafter the legitimacy of the Mixed Court and of its proceedings in terms of Western jurisprudence and Western concepts of international relations is open to serious challenge and few responsible authorities have attempted to sustain it.

Most Western writers have either ignored the issue or skated carefully around it. Some have frankly acknowledged the weakness of the court's foundation. Anatol M. Kotenev never attempted to justify the court's jurisdiction in terms of any principles drawn from jurisprudence. He appealed instead to history and to "the law of historical necessity." "The existing status of the International Mixed Court," he wrote, "is nothing more than the natural result of an unavoidable historical process." He claimed that it was not the willful contempt of the foreigners but "an immutable law of logic which has forced the Chinese nation to give up a part of its sovereign right."[4]

Escarra did not attempt to justify the legitimacy of the court in the hands of the consuls after the recognition of the Republic of China by the treaty powers in 1913. On the contrary, he acknowledged and deplored what he saw as the conditions of arbitrariness, irregularity, and illegality under which the court carried on its work.[5]

The International Commission on Extraterritoriality in China, in its report of September 1926, expressly refrained from offering any opinion on the status of the court under the consuls. The commission contented itself with noting that the position of the court was anomalous, that "as at present constituted it has been functioning without treaty sanction since October 1911," and that its rendition to Chinese control was under discussion.[6]

Westel Willoughby did not attempt to invoke any principles of jurisprudence upon which to support the court, but appealed instead to "practical administrative efficiency" as the justification for its proceedings under the consuls. He wrote:

> Regarded from a strictly legal point of view it is impossible to justify [the] refusal of the powers to yield to the several times expressed request of the Peking government that Chinese control should be reestablished. Regarded however from the viewpoint of practical administrative efficiency the powers have felt themselves justified in retaining their control until the Chinese Government should be willing to agree to certain reforms which the powers deemed essential to the efficient working of the court.[7]

INFRINGEMENT OF CHINESE SOVEREIGNTY

The challenge to the validity of the Mixed Court's proceedings after 1911 arises, of course, out of the doctrines of the inviolability of the territorial sovereignty of states in Western concepts of international relations. According to these principles:

The jurisdiction of the nation within its own territory is necessarily exclusive and absolute. It is susceptible of no limitation not imposed by itself. . . . All exceptions therefore to the full and complete power of a nation within its own territories must be traced up to the consent of the nation itself. They can flow from no other legitimate source.[8]

The necessary consent to the sovereign limitation may be evidenced by express treaty or may be inferred from sufferance.[9] The Mixed Court after 1911 could claim neither. Its constitution and its operation were outside and beyond the provisions of any treaty and were consistently objected to rather than assented to or acquiesced in by the Republic of China. No long period of usage could be claimed. On the contrary, the surrender of the control of the court had in the first place been forced upon China against its will by an aggressive consular body backed by the threat of the superior military power of the treaty nations. Throughout the long and futile negotiations for the return of the court the Chinese never withdrew their demand for its return and never came to any agreement that would allow the consuls to retain it.

In the absence of treaty rights or assent and acquiescence over a long period of usage, the establishment and conduct on Chinese soil of a court for the trial and punishment of Chinese citizens within their own territory and for the enforcement in China of claims against Chinese by foreigners can hardly be seen in Western theory as anything other than an illegitimate arrogation by the consuls of Chinese sovereign powers.

The British government was of course not unaware of the weakness of the court's foundation, and when challenged in Parliament, the Foreign Secretary endeavored to justify the situation in the only way justification could arise: by alleging consent of the sovereign power impinged upon. In July 1925 the matter of consular control over the Mixed Court was raised in the House of Commons when the question was asked, what treaty or agreement gives to the consuls at Shanghai the power to appoint the judges of the Mixed Court without reference to the Chinese government? The Foreign Secretary replied that the practice was established in 1911 and "was confirmed by the declaration made by Yuan Shih-k'ai on his recognition as President of the Republic of China."[10] This was a reference to a passage in a speech made by Yuan Shikai on 10 October 1913, the occasion of the recognition by the great powers of the Republic of China and of himself as its president. Yuan said:

I hereby declare that all treaties, conventions, and international agreements entered into between the former Manchu and Provisional Republican Governments, of the one part, and the foreign Governments of the other part, shall be strictly observed . . . and further that all rights privileges and immunities enjoyed by foreigners in China by virtue of international engagements, national enactments, and established usages are hereby confirmed.[11]

This passage was dictated by the treaty powers and inserted in Yuan's speech at their insistence. They refused to grant recognition to his government or the Republic of China unless and until he publicly made this declaration.[12]

It is not easy, however, to see how this declaration could be taken to confirm consular control of the Mixed Court. There certainly was no treaty, international agreement or engagement, or national enactment that gave the consuls control of the court. The only words that might be relevant to the Mixed Court situation are "established usages." But it is very difficult to argue seriously that a temporary arrangement made in a time of emergency which had now passed, supported by threat of force against the will of local and government authorities, and of only two years' duration, could be an established usage within the meaning of the declaration. It may much more cogently be argued that the words "established usage" in the context of the recognition of a new regime were obviously directed to usages established during the previously recognized Manzhou regime.

Nevertheless the Foreign Secretary's reply in 1925 appears to have satisfied the House. Whether his reply would have satisfied the Privy Council may be doubted. It is certain that it would not have satisfied the Supreme Court of China.

THE DECISION OF THE CHINESE SUPREME COURT

In 1917 the judges of the Supreme Court of China applying the principles of Western jurisprudence had no difficulty in arriving at the conclusion that the conduct of the Mixed Court under consular control since 1911 had no warranty in the provisions of any treaty and that the Chinese government had never recognized the validity of its condition under the consuls. Consequently, the Supreme Court declared:

The Mixed Court clearly is not a part of the ordinary judicial system of China. A case may, *de facto*, be determined judicially without such decision being considered as having legal effect. A case therefore which has been decided in the Mixed Court may be tried by Judicial Courts of competent jurisdiction elsewhere in China, and a plea of *res adjudicata* cannot be entertained. As to decisions in criminal cases . . . the defendant is to be considered as not having had a trial by a court of competent jurisdiction and the Public Procurator may prosecute such cases in order to maintain the dignity of the law and for the public good.[13]

This denial of legitimacy and recognition to the judgments of the Mixed Court was ignored by the Mixed Court itself but was taken very seriously by the diplomatic body and particularly by the Americans. Allman in 1922 stressed the necessity of making it a condition of any return of the court to Chinese control that the judgments of the court should be validated and should be recognized and given effect to by all Chinese courts in the republic.[14] Schurman, the American minister, advised Washington in March 1924 that rendition should only be upon a condition "that all Mixed Court decisions will be recognized and given effect by all Chinese courts throughout the Republic."[15] The Americans took the view that unless this was done "all judgments over 16 years would be capable of being set aside and reopened."[16]

In the end, both upon the abolition of the Mixed Court in favor of the Provisional Court of Jiangsu in 1927 and upon the takeover of the Provisional Court of Jiangsu by the Special District Court of Shanghai in 1930, a provision was included in the arrangements validating the process and the judgments of the Mixed Court throughout China.

But notwithstanding the grave doubts as to whether the Mixed Court had any legitimate basis for the jurisdiction it exercised, and notwithstanding the declaration of the Supreme Court of China in 1917 that it did not, and that it was not a court at all and its decisions were of no legal effect, and notwithstanding the anxiety this situation gave rise to in diplomatic circles, nevertheless the Mixed Court continued to operate very successfully, to expand, and to grow. It handled millions of dollars worth of disputed claims and came to be referred to as "the most powerful court in the world."[17] On the criminal side it did not hesitate to deal with capital cases and sent hundreds of men and some women to execution. It sent thousands of offenders to prison, many for twenty years and some for life. It exercised an unlimited jurisdiction both as to subject matter and as to amount claimed. There was no appeal from its decisions.

How then, it may be asked, could the Mixed Court achieve this success, how could it even survive, when the very basis of its constitution was so precarious and the legality of its proceedings so questionable? If the court's constitution should be held to be unsound and invalid, then the Chinese magistrates, the foreign assessors who participated in the court's judgments, the court officials, the municipal council, and the municipal police who executed their judgments were all acting arbitrarily and without jurisdiction and were liable to heavy damages, and all the proceedings of the court were null and void. How did the court survive? It is instructive to examine this question first in the light of Western legal principles and then in the light of the principles of disciplinary theory.

THE WESTERN LEGAL VIEW

In the eyes of the Western lawyer the seizure by the foreign consuls of control of the Mixed Court and its punitive and disciplinary functions in respect to Chinese citizens appeared as acts of sovereign power on the part of the states that the consuls represented. An act of sovereign power in respect to foreign relations and committed outside the state, called an "act of state" is not challengeable in the municipal courts of the state.[18]

It is to be borne in mind that owing to the incidence of extraterritoriality, any action against any treaty power assessor, court official, or police officer could only be brought in his own national court. Thus a British assessor or a British police officer could only be attacked in a British court. Such an attack would be met by the defense of "act of state." One of the cluster of principles enforced in the administration of the doctrines of act of state in the courts of Great Britain is that a person who is not under allegiance to the Crown cannot be permitted to use the courts of the Crown to condemn the acts of the Crown, that is acts of state, outside the realm. "What the Crown does to foreigners by its agents without the realm, is State action also, and is beyond the scope of domestic jurisdiction," said Lord Sumner.[19] Thus no Chinese national could be heard in any British court to say that the acts of the Crown in setting up and operating the Mixed Court in China were wrongful so as to give him any right of recourse in the courts of the Crown against anybody. The protection extends to cover all persons concerned in effectuating the act of state. In the period 1911–27 perhaps the best judicial treatment of the subject in England was the judgment of Lord Justice Fletcher Moulton in *Salaman v. Secretary of State for India*. He said:

An act of State is essentially an exercise of sovereign power, and hence cannot be challenged, controlled or interfered with by municipal Courts. Its sanction is not that of law, but that of sovereign power, and, whatever it be, municipal courts must accept it as it is without question. But it may and often must, be part of their duty to take cognizance of it. . . . The rights accruing therefrom may have to be adjudicated upon by municipal Courts. . . . In deciding on such a claim the Courts must loyally accept the act of State as effective.[20]

It follows, in relation to the Mixed Court, that all British courts in Shanghai and elsewhere, including the Privy Council, were compelled to look upon the Mixed Court and its process as properly constituted and possessed of whatever jurisdiction and authority in respect of Chinese nationals the consuls, as agents for their sovereigns, cared to vest in it. Such jurisdiction had to be taken as valid and not open to attack, and so far as I have been able to discover no such attack was ever attempted.

As for any attack on the municipal council for its part in the operations of the Mixed Court, such attack would have to be made in the court of consuls. Here again, no one could expect to be allowed to use a court composed of the consuls of the treaty powers to condemn the acts of the treaty powers performed through the agency of the consuls. The court of consuls was not bound by the transcendent imperatives of any sovereign or other power external to itself, but came to its own conclusions upon whatever principles it saw fit to apply. There was no appeal.

But the effect of the doctrine of Act of State in a British court is not to justify the act nor to make right the wrong. The act remains a wrong. The effect is simply to preclude any person who may have been wronged from claiming any remedy for that wrong in any British court. Lord Atkinson put it thus:

It is on the authorities quite clear that the injury inflicted upon an individual by the act of State of a sovereign authority does not by reason of the nature of the act by which the injury is inflicted cease to be a wrong. What these authorities do establish is that a remedy for the wrong cannot be sought for in the Courts of the sovereign authority which inflicts the injury, and that the aggrieved party must depend for redress upon the diplomatic action of the State of which he is a subject.[21]

Thus, looking through Western spectacles, we arrive at the rather unsatisfactory result that, according to the principles of Western jurisprudence, while the Mixed Court and its jurisdiction over Chinese nationals after 1911 probably did not derive from Chinese sovereign power at all but appear rather to have been arbitrary, improper, wrong, and contrary both to the rules and conventions of international relations and to the internal domestic rules and imperatives of the treaty powers, no Chinese national was permitted to prove this, nor even to test it, in any British court. Similar considerations and restrictions applied in the courts of other treaty powers.[22]

THE CHINESE DISCIPLINARY VIEW

When we look at the Mixed Court, however, in the light of disciplinary principles, as the Shanghai Chinese saw it, a totally different picture emerges. But to see this picture we are required to do something that, as has already been suggested, may be very difficult for Westerners and particularly Western lawyers to do. We are required to cease thinking and reasoning in terms of the familiar Western legal order and to commence thinking and *feeling* in terms of disciplinary concepts of order instead. If we can do this the picture clears at once.

In disciplinary systems, as we have seen, jurisdiction or rather its analogous concept in disciplinary theory, better called "competence," is not a question of law but a question of fact.[23] Let us consider some facts. The International Settlement at Shanghai constituted a readily identifiable group-community, clearly defined and sharply differentiated from any other group in China. It had specific and readily identifiable leaders in the consular body and the municipal council to whom all looked for direction, protection, and control. When either of these issued a proclamation or an ordinance they had power to compel obedience, since they controlled the application of force. The municipal council controlled the police and the Shanghai Volunteer Corps. Behind the consuls representing the treaty powers, there loomed the formidable threat of the combined armies and navies of Europe, the United States, and Japan. The consuls and the council also had the power to enforce the characteristic sanction of all disciplinary groups: expulsion of offenders from the group to fend for themselves in a hostile world outside the protection of the group. Under these circumstances it was clearly competent for the leaders of the group, indeed it was expected of them in disciplinary theory, that they should set up machinery for the maintenance of order, for dispute resolution, and for the punishment of wrongdoing and disobedience of orders. If the consuls chose, as they did, to do this by setting up a tribunal, and if the municipal council chose, as it did, to manage the affairs of that tribunal and to place the police force at its disposal, then nothing more was required. The tribunal had in fact competence to maintain order and settle disputes. To the Chinese in Shanghai, thinking in terms of disciplinary theory, the question of whether the Mixed Court had jurisdiction in accordance with the principles of Western jurisprudence was simply irrelevant. There was no point in asking it.[24] In disciplinary theory one does not think in terms of the transcendent rigid imperatives of Western jurisprudence. It is characteristic of disciplinary systems that the policy and the instructions of the leaders of the immediate group take precedence over the pronouncements and edicts, and even the legislative prescriptions, of the more remote central power.[25] In the *Ming Sung Umbrella* case in 1926 at Shanghai a witness was asked: "Do you obey the judgment or decisions of your own Supreme Court or do you not?" and he replied "If it is reasonable I will obey; if it is not I will not obey." Further cross-examination made it clear that by "reasonable" he meant in accordance with the policies of his merchant guild in Shanghai.[26]

THE DECISION OF THE SUPREME COURT DISCOUNTED

In view of the operation of this principle it is not surprising that any attempt by a litigant to take advantage of the Supreme Court ruling of 1917 by bringing again, outside the settlement, an action he had lost within it, was severely discouraged not only within the settlement but by courts outside it. On 29 May 1919 one H. Robertson commenced proceedings in the Shanghai District Court for the rehearing of a matter which had been heard and determined by the Mixed Court in 1911. When this was reported to Grant Jones, the senior British assessor, he promptly took action. What he did is not recorded, but the result was that, on 10 June, Robertson's summons was dismissed by the Shanghai District Court as "irregular procedure."[27] The inference to be drawn from this is that the arrangement between the Shanghai District Court outside the settlement and the Mixed Court within it for the reciprocal execution of each other's process was too valuable to the district court to risk the loss of it by refusing recognition to the Mixed Court's judgment, whatever the Supreme Court in distant Beijing might say. Conformably to group disciplinary practice, the Supreme Court judgment carried only such force in the courts of Shanghai city as the judges of those courts cared to give it, having regard first to local circumstances and requirements.

In another case, in 1925, one Kao Yao-ding, having failed to succeed in an action in the Mixed Court against Zee Van-kao, took his action again in the district court of the Chinese city outside settlement limits.

Here, by misleading the court, he got a judgment by default against Zee, lured Zee out of the settlement into the city, and had him arrested and thrown into prison. There Zee was detained for about a month and was compelled to pay the full amount of Kao's claim before he could secure his release and return to the safety of the settlement.

When these facts were laid before the consuls and the municipal council, Kao was prosecuted for contempt of court. He raised the defense that the Mixed Court judgment was not a bar to his pursuing the same claim again in the courts outside the settlement, but he was convicted and sentenced to two months' imprisonment. The assessor said that this kind of case was uncommon "but in the event of its repetition the sentence would be a long one and would involve expulsion."[28]

A CHINESE JUDGE'S APPROACH

It is difficult for a Western lawyer to *feel* instinctively, as disciplinary theory requires, that this principle of the overriding authority of the de facto leaders of the immediate group is a natural one, therefore right and proper and not open to question, but it is not difficult for a Chinese to do so. Discipline is a state of mind, and group-disciplinary principles have been deeply engrained and relentlessly inculcated in the traditional thought and culture patterns of the Chinese for centuries, indeed for millennia. It is hardly surprising therefore that such principles will often be found to strike a responsive chord in the mind of a Chinese—even in the mind of a Western-trained Chinese lawyer, and even today—more readily and more immediately than will the exotic, unwelcome, and unnatural concepts of Western legal systems. This approach appeared clearly enough in a personal interview of September 1979 with a retired Chinese judge. He was a judge who had lived, and occupied a place on the bench, in the Shanghai of the late nineteen-twenties. I asked him, If the Supreme Court of China had declared unequivocally that the Mixed Court was not lawfully constituted and had no jurisdiction, and that its decisions were nullities, how did it survive? How could it maintain any shred of credibility or respectability in legal circles? The judge I was questioning was a distinguished Chinese lawyer who had taken his degree of J.D. at Michigan Law School. He was well aware of the situation of the Mixed Court at first hand. He had been in fact one of the judges of the Provisional Court of Jiangsu, which took over the work of the Mixed Court when it was abolished in 1927. He seemed mildly surprised at my question and replied that the magistrate Guan Jiong was honest, he was well-liked and respected by the Chinese and by the foreign community, his judgments were fair, and they were enforced. "What more do you want? What more is necessary?" he asked.

The judge's mind was of course working in terms of disciplinary theory in the context of the group-structured society of Shanghai and the settlement. The notion that any reference might be necessary to an outside code of the rigid, universal imperatives of some transcendent national or sovereign power to justify the act or the order of a de facto authority in a group was simply not there. It is significant that the Provisional Court of Jiangsu, the judge's own former court, could itself claim no more constitutional validity, no greater legitimacy, and no sounder legal jurisdiction than the Mixed Court could. The Provisional Court of Jiangsu was no more the creation of the sovereign power, and no more a creature of the constitution, than the Mixed Court had been. Like the Mixed Court, it was sired by military might and born of disciplinary theory, but the judge thought none the less of it for that and felt honored to take a seat on its bench. Like the Mixed Court, the provisional court was simply the creation of the leaders of a group, in this case the warlord Sun Chuanfang and his advisers, rulers de facto of the Jiangsu-Zhejiang-Anhui-Jiangxi-Fujian group of provinces.

THE CONSULS' COUP REPEATED BY THE WARLORD

There were some striking resemblances between the two cases. When the consuls acted in Shanghai in 1911, the central government in Beijing, the Manzhou regime, was failing. Within a few months it flickered out and died. When Sun Chuanfang acted in 1926, the central government in Beijing was again failing. Within a few months it had flickered out and died. By the time the Provisional Court of Jiangsu was constituted and held its first sitting in January 1927, there was no central government in Beijing nor anywhere else in China. China's sovereignty meant nothing. There was nobody to exercise it. China's constitution meant nothing. It had been repeatedly violated by successive Chinese governments and in the end it had been expressly abrogated. It was Sun Chuanfang who did, on this occasion, what the consuls had done in 1911—stepped into the power vacuum and, by his mere fiat as leader of a local group, without any sovereign, constitutional, or other legal warranty, erected a court within the settlement competent to maintain order and resolve disputes. Moreover Sun Chuanfang's creation, the provisional court, had this advantage, in 1927, over the consul's creation, the Mixed Court: the provisional court could command what the Mixed Court had lost, recognition by and the cooperation of the

Chinese courts operating in other groups outside the settlement area. This gave it that breadth of geographic competence the loss of which had crippled the usefulness of the Mixed Court.

SUMMATION

Summing up, then, the questions of the basic authority of the Mixed Court after 1911 and where it got its authority from, we may say that this matter responds much more simply, directly, and profitably to treatment in terms of disciplinary theory than in terms of Western jurisprudence. It is certain that the Chinese saw it and interpreted it instinctively in terms of disciplinary theory, although of course they were not then in a position to identify it *eo nomine* and to articulate it as disciplinary theory. The claim of the court to legitimacy in terms of Western jurisprudence raises many difficulties and problems. We are left in the unhappy situation that the Chinese Supreme Court declared unequivocally that the Mixed Court had none, while the British and American courts were not permitted to consider the matter or to offer any opinion on it. In terms of disciplinary theory, however, all is plain sailing and no problems arise. The claim of the court to competence was a simple question of fact and could not be denied. The court showed its competence daily. Within the settlement, its orders were final and were instantly enforced without question. Outside the area controlled by the municipal police, the court attained competence by the device of refusing execution within the settlement of Chinese process originated outside it except on terms of reciprocity, that is to say unless Mixed Court process was recognized and executed by Chinese instrumentalities outside the settlement. This worked until 1925, when reciprocity was withdrawn by the outside authorities. The result of this withdrawal was that the court's sphere of competence contracted to the area of the settlement, and its usefulness was so severely impaired that in 1926 the consuls agreed to its abolition. Its place was taken by a court that could command a sphere of competence extending far beyond the limits of the settlement.

PRINCIPLES GUIDING MIXED COURT DECISIONS

We turn now to the question, Upon what principles did the Mixed Court act in the performance of its functions after 1911?

In imperial times Chinese officials charged with the settlement of disputes and the maintenance of order were not expected to act impartially as independent judges in the adjudicative mode. They were required to act as subordinate agencies of the imperial court, enforcing discipline on behalf of and in the interests of imperial authority, and they were subject to direction accordingly. The Mixed Court in imperial times, in spite of all the assessors could do, never lost this character.

How did it act under consular control? Did it follow and apply impartially any coherent body of explicit rules, and if so where did it get them, and upon what system did it recognize them? How far, on the other hand, did the court continue to act at large doing whatever it thought best in the interests of the group-community and in the furtherance of the group leaders' policies, taking direction from the group leaders accordingly?

THE "LAWS OF CHINA"

There was a short and convenient formula always ready to hand for answering—or at least smothering—these questions, to which the court itself and those writing about the court often had recourse. It was to say that the court was a Chinese court and that therefore, subject to some minor reservations and modifications, it was bound by and applied "the laws of China."

Thus a Foreign Office memorandum of 1925 on "The Administration of Justice in Shanghai" referring to the Mixed Court declared that "Chinese law, modified to a certain extent by foreign procedure, is the law of the court."[29] Jacobs, the American assessor, describing the court as it was in 1923, said, "The law applied is still Chinese law except in the case of Russian defendants for whom Russian law applies."[30]

In the case of *The Gold and Silversmiths Guild v. The Shanghai Municipal Police* in 1912, Grant Jones, British assessor, delivering judgment said "By treaty and by International law, this court must be guided by the law of the defendant's nationality, that is by the law of China."[31] In 1925, in *Ex Parte Zung*, Arthur J. Martin, British assessor, said in effect that the court was bound to apply whatever Chinese laws were in force. The magistrate, Guan Jiong, "concurred, emphasising that persons brought up at court must be dealt with according to the laws of the Republic of China."[32]

But for our purposes to say that the Mixed Court applied the "laws of China" is merely begging the question. It only substitutes another question: What is meant by that glib phrase "the laws of China," or, more particularly, What specific significance, if any, can be spelled out of the expression "the laws of China" in the context of the China of 1911–27?

The International Commission on Extraterritoriality was called upon in 1925, to investigate at some length the nature of "the laws of China." The American view was expressed by Joseph E. Jacobs, senior American assessor and legal adviser to the American commissioner Silas H. Strawn. Jacobs submitted a written opinion to his commissioner concluding that:

> In the strict sense of the word, therefore, neither the laws of China nor the Provisional Government itself have any legal basis for existence. The laws exist by virtue of Presidential Mandates or Ministerial Orders of governments recognizing the Provisional Constitution of 1912 which contained no authority for such a method of enacting law, and, furthermore, whatever authority might have existed under that Provisional Constitution has certainly now lapsed since it has been set aside by the present Provisional Government which functions without a Constitution.[33]

This lack of any constitutional basis for "the laws of China" was put squarely before the Chinese commissioner Wang Chonghui for explanation. Wang had no difficulty at all relapsing at once into the same type of disciplinary thinking that we have previously noticed in the Shanghai judge, namely that once a de facto authority promulgates an edict it is effective and will be enforced by the courts, and that "the question of constitutionality does not arise." In China, Wang observed, laws are enforced when they are properly promulgated.

> A court of law if it feels called upon to consider the legality of a statute will not go beyond the inquiry whether or not the same has been duly promulgated by the proper authorities. . . . Although from the foreign point of view the validity of the recent Chinese legislation may be considered debatable the Chinese themselves have never had any doubt as to the propriety of enforcing the said legislation. In fact the bulk of the laws, ordinances, mandates, regulations and rules enacted since the establishment of the Republic by the Parliament, by the President, by the Chief executive and by the various Ministries acting alone or in conjunction have been regularly published in the Government Gazette and on such promulgation have been considered by the Courts as perfectly valid.[34]

In the result the commission reported that although under the Chinese constitution it was clear that the sole law-making body in China was parliament, nevertheless the great bulk of the material placed before it as "the laws of China" had never been enacted nor confirmed by parliament. The "laws" were comprised of directives, orders, commands, and mandates issued by the president and by the minister for justice. These were amendable and revocable by the president and by the minister at will. Under the constitution neither the president nor the minister had any legislative authority. The commission further reported that the enforcement of these orders and mandates was not universal but varied very much in scope and effectiveness from time to time and from place to place. Enforcement depended on the attitudes of provincial governors, local rulers, and group leaders. Throughout most parts of China the local rulers and authorities were accustomed to issue their own mandates and edicts for obedience in their own districts, and these might or might not correspond with those issued from Beijing. Large areas of China were governed by provincial authorities who refused recognition to the central government, and who promulgated their own "laws," that is, mandates and ordinances.[35]

The commission decided arbitrarily that it would in its report use the expression "law" to cover the mandates, orders, and directives issued from Beijing but not those issued by provincial authorities.[36] This summary way of determining which mandates were law and which were not, while tidy and convenient in theory, was far from realistic in fact, if by *law* we mean rules prescribing conduct. It was a time when the edicts of provincial authorities were undoubtedly far more effective in constraining conduct over a much greater area of China than the edicts that issued from Beijing. The area controlled by Beijing commenced shrinking and continued to shrink progressively from about 1917.

From 1920 the fragmentation of China and the deterioration in the authority of the central government proceeded at an accelerated pace. On 29 November 1921 the *North-China Daily News* reported:

> The Central Government still sits in Peking amidst the Imperial palaces, grown dusty and disreputable. It still issues eloquent and empty proclamations. But its writ does not run much farther than the city gates. In Manchuria a little satrap has set up for himself. Most of the provinces have declared their independence. Sun Wen and his Rump Parliament sit in Canton and more or less rule the South.[37]

In 1926 central government finally collapsed altogether, and nothing took its place. There was then no central government in Beijing nor anywhere else in China to enforce the laws if there were any.

But even assuming a central sovereign government in China, and even accepting its mandates and edicts as law, there still remained, the commission found, a number of important matters affecting the rights and obligations of citizens "in regard to which no laws existed." These included matters usually dealt with in a civil code, such as obligations, things, family and domestic relations, succession and inheritance, and matters usually dealt with in a commercial code, such as negotiable instruments, banking, insurance, partnerships, insolvents, and so on.[38] In such matters the courts were permitted, and indeed exhorted, by the Supreme Court to apply custom, and in the absence of custom "general legal principles." What general legal principles meant, or where one was to go for them, was nowhere specified.[39]

Further the commission found that very often the decisive factor in prescribing the conduct expected of citizens was not "the laws of China" nor any of the matters that we have been discussing so far but military power. The commission found that the device of martial law, that is the enforcement of the mere will of the local military commander, was being so extensively employed and abused that it constituted a grave menace to the proper administration of civil order in China. Military leaders, said the commission, "possessing as they do their own armies engaged in constant war-fare, exercise almost unrestrained authority over the lives, liberty and property of the people in the area which happen for the time being to be within their control."[40]

Under all these circumstances it will have become apparent that our quest for "the laws of China" has degenerated into nothing more than an exercise in "backward translation," the process of starting with the English words and then striving desperately to find something, somewhere, in the Chinese scene to which the phrase can, however inaptly and inappropriately, be attached. It is with relief that we remember that the Chinese system in all its manifestations and variety was a disciplinary one and that disciplinary theory finds no use for the word or the idiom of "law."

ORDER WITHOUT LAW

The attempt therefore to find any specific feature of the maintenance of order in the China of 1911–27 that might usefully or helpfully be labeled "law" will be abandoned. This means that the question before us reverts to its original form: Upon what principles did the Mixed Court act after 1911 in coming to its decisions? If it applied rules, what were they, where did it get them from, and upon what compulsions did it recognize and accept them?

It may be said at once, as the Commission on Extraterritoriality found, that there was not in existence in China in the period 1911–27 any such comprehensive body of predetermined universal and transcendent imperatives administered by a sovereign power as is required to provide the essential basis for the operation of an adjudicative system of the type so familiar to students of dispute resolution and social order in the West. Only in theory could the China of 1911–27 be regarded as a homogeneous state under a central sovereign power. In actuality it consisted of a congeries of autonomous groups loosely associated in common cultural traditions and sometimes linked in fragile political alliances, but more often in competition and frequently in a state of actual war with one another.

Within the group a citizen's primary obligation was to obey the commands of the immediate superior and to carry out the orders and support the policies of the group leader. There were no codes of rules transcending both the citizen and the will of the group leader.

Nevertheless a large body of written material in the shape of mandates, edicts, and codes of standing orders, regulations, and directives on a variety of specific if disconnected topics was originated and promulgated by various authorities at various levels in various groups throughout China from time to time. Georges Padoux published in 1936 a list of 234 such sets of mandates and edicts emanating from the Beijing command between 1911 and 1927 and available in translation in a European language.[41] This of course was only a tiny fraction of the number issued from Beijing and remaining untranslated and of the number issued by authorities independent of Beijing throughout the rest of China. Some of these mandates and orders had a possible application to matters coming before the Mixed Court, but the great majority of them were only of local significance.

These mandates and orders were, as the theory of disciplinary systems recognizes, effective only to the extent that the authority issuing them could physically enforce them, or that local group leaders chose to adopt and enforce any of them within their local group.[42] Accordingly, within the International Settlement, the imperative force of any mandate, order, or pronouncement depended upon the degree to which the consuls, the municipal council, and their order-enforcement tribunal, the Mixed Court, were prepared to recognize and enforce it.

Thus no levy of any Chinese taxation whether on foreigners or on Chinese was effective within the settlement unless the consuls approved and permitted it. So, again, no effect was given within the settlement to the decision of the Supreme Court of China that the Mixed Court was without jurisdiction and illegal. The group simply did not recognize the judgment and it remained a dead letter. In 1925 in *Ex parte Zung Pao-lai* the Mixed Court was moved for a declaration that "The Law of Publication" of 1914 should not be recognized or enforced within the settlement. After argument and some consideration the court refused the application, but it might as easily have granted it.[43] In 1922 the postal commissioner at Shanghai advised the senior British assessor Blackburn that some new postal regulations had been promulgated and inquired if the Mixed Court would recognize them. Blackburn replied

> I have talked the matter over with the Senior Magistrate and with my American colleague and can see no objection to the enforcement of the laws in question in the Mixed Court. We will enforce them on receiving an official copy of the text.[44]

Thus the mandates, standing orders, and directives of Chinese authority were by no means always imperative upon the Mixed Court and did not constitute such a body of ineluctable rules as the assessors needed and as Western jurisprudence demands for the foundation of a true adjudicative system. Nevertheless the assessors were able to use some of this material very conveniently, and, as they hoped, convincingly, to serve their purposes. For, whenever the court in giving judgment followed the mandates or codes of standing orders of any superior authority, it appeared, or could be made to appear, that the court was not acting arbitrarily but was bound by and was enforcing known and coercive rules in the manner of adjudicative systems. Using this material the assessors, dedicated to the ideals of Western jurisprudence and having no other framework of theory to follow, labored earnestly and sincerely to establish in the Mixed Court the principles of the adjudicative mode, and most of the time truly believed in their own minds that they were succeeding.

Of all the material that the assessors were accustomed to draw upon to justify their decisions, two sets of rules and regulations in particular proved the most useful and were the most frequently invoked. These were the corpus of rules comprised in the land regulations and byelaws[45] and in the ordinances, proclamations, and notifications of the municipal council,[46] and the corpus of rules comprising the Provisional Criminal Code. Indeed it may be said that the primary function for which the Mixed Court existed in this period was to maintain order in the settlement in the terms of, or at least guided by, the provisions of these two sets of rules insofar as such provisions were consonant with consular policy and direction. Neither set of rules was up-to-date or complete, neither fully met European ideals, and neither was the legislative act of any sovereign power. But each had been formally promulgated by an acknowledged superior authority in the hierarchical and disciplinary society of China, and accordingly the application of them as compulsory was accepted by all subordinate Chinese without a murmur. They offered therefore a reasonable substitute for Western codes of transcendent universal imperatives of conduct and could be treated and used by the assessors (with some reservations) as imperative rules in terms of which to develop adjudicative processes in the Mixed Court.

THE LAND REGULATIONS AND BYELAWS

As for the land regulations, it is true that the legal status of these in relation to treaty power nationals was always open to doubt and subject to challenge in Western courts. As early as 1865 their enforceability in terms of Western jurisprudence was disputed in Her Britannic Majesty's Supreme Court for China.[47] As late as 1925, Judge Purdy in the United States Court for China expressed grave doubt whether, as a matter of law, they could be enforced against a United States citizen, and he only enforced them reluctantly for reasons of expediency and not of law.[48]

But so far as the Chinese before the Mixed Court were concerned, no such difficulties arose. As far back as 1855 obedience to the land regulations had been enjoined by proclamation of the Daotai upon all Chinese resorting to the settlement.[49] In 1899 new land regulations and byelaws were promulgated by the Daotai and obedience both to the old and to the new was commanded by his proclamation.[50] In the minds of the Chinese, thinking and feeling in terms of disciplinary theory, this was all that was required. Immediate superior authority had spoken, and no one needed anything more than that. The Chinese magistrates of the Mixed Court never showed any hesitation in enforcing the regulations and the Chinese defendants never showed any disposition to question their binding force.

THE PROVISIONAL CRIMINAL CODE

The Provisional Criminal Code of the Republic of China arose out of a draft prepared in imperial times by the Commissioners for the Revision of the Laws and presented to the throne in 1907. This draft, which gave rise to much controversy, was revised and re-presented in 1910 but was never actually promulgated by the imperial court. However, after the abdication of the emperor in February 1912, Yuan Shikai, by his mandate of 10 March 1912 as president of China, promulgated the revised draft provisionally as the criminal code of the republic.

By this mandate the president proclaimed:

> Whereas the laws of the republic have not yet been promulgated it is hereby ordered that all the laws previously in force and the Provisional Criminal Code shall for the time being be applicable; provided that such articles as are repugnant to the republican form of government shall be void.[51]

The assessors of the Mixed Court in the International Settlement found that although the code was incomplete and defective in many respects, its provisions were in general suitable for their purposes and convenient for the conduct of the criminal proceedings of the Mixed Court. Accordingly they brought it into general use and the municipal police, whenever they could, framed their criminal charges as breaches of its provisions. This did not mean, of course, that the assessors accepted the code as invariably binding upon the court. On the contrary, they were quite prepared to depart from it when they thought the interests of the settlement and the policies of its leaders demanded a departure. Thus when the consuls and the municipal council were trying to suppress the opium trade, the court took the view that the maximum fine allowed by the code for possession and sale of opium, five hundred dollars, was not enough. The court accordingly proceeded to inflict fines of thousands of dollars in many cases, far in excess of the maximum permitted under the code.[52]

Nevertheless insofar as the Mixed Court chose to enforce the provisions of the code, it could be and was represented and used by the assessors as a code of imperatives in terms of which to practice, and to demonstrate the characteristics of, adjudicative processes of forensic science.

Thus, the land regulations and byelaws, the ordinances, proclamations, and notifications of the municipal council and the Provisional Criminal Code taken together provided a corpus of rules sufficient to support the great bulk of the work of the Mixed Court on the criminal side, that is to say the disposal of charges of municipal offenses, police offenses, and criminal offenses of all kinds, great and small. On the civil side it was much more difficult to find specific imperative rules upon which to found adjudicative decisions. In family and commercial affairs custom, group propriety, and group leadership directives were the primary determinants in dispute resolution. Except in some narrow and technical areas such as incorporated associations, copyright, and trademarks, preordained and imperative rules in civil and business matters were almost entirely lacking. There was nothing approaching the comprehensive cover of a civil or commercial code.

DECISION IN CIVIL PROCEEDINGS

Under these circumstances the court invoked in civil cases, when it could, three main sources to justify its decisions in the adjudicative manner. The first was the mandate of Yuan Shikai of 1912 referred to above. This was read as preserving such parts of the *Da Qing Lu Li* as related to civil and not to criminal affairs. Just which parts were preserved was never spelled out, but clearly they were few and far between. The *Da Qing Lu Li* was essentially a code of criminal sanctions, and provisions regulating civil affairs were conspicuous only by their absence. Nevertheless the code could sometimes be appealed to in such matters as marriage, concubinage, child adoption, succession, and so on, particularly in purely Chinese cases.

The second source was the various series of published decisions and interpretations of the Supreme Court of China.[53] Just what weight was required to be given to these decisions and interpretations by inferior Chinese courts was not beyond argument.[54] Nevertheless, the Supreme Court often followed in trade disputes modern commercial and legal practice in Western countries, and its decisions and interpretations could sometimes be drawn upon to provide an authority upon which to base a Mixed Court judgment.

The third and perhaps the most flexible and useful authority upon which the Mixed Court could rely in civil cases was a decision of the Supreme Court of China given in 1913. This decision is generally quoted, in translation, in the following form:

> Civil cases are decided first according to express provisions of law; in the absence of express provisions, then according to customs, and, in the absence of customs, then in accordance with legal principles.[55]

The phrase "legal principles," however, here offered as a translation of the Chinese characters *tiao li*, 條理, smacks somewhat of backward translation. The Chinese could be better rendered "right principles of regular order" and the passage better understood as conveying the idea of "what are generally acknowledged by common agreement to be the best principles to apply in such cases in the interests of regularity and order."[56] In any case the phrase is splendidly vague and gave the Mixed Court a wide latitude.

Many of the commercial cases before the Mixed Court concerned modern trade practices that were unknown in Chinese custom and not regulated by any written code. The court therefore could follow European precedents and still claim by virtue of this ruling to be following the Supreme Court of China.[57] Under the same ruling it was possible for the Mixed Court sometimes to invoke as "legal principles" the provisions of the draft civil code prepared in 1911 and to rest its decisions on them long before the code was promulgated in 1929–31.[58] So also the court could treat as "legal principles," and use as an authority the old bankruptcy code long after it was abrogated in 1908.[59]

Thus, going for supplies of rules to the various sources that have been mentioned, the Mixed Court was able most of the time to reflect in its proceedings the adjudicative mode and to relate its decisions to some written provision or another, somewhere, that could be made to do duty as a predetermined inexorable imperative.

DISCIPLINARY PRINCIPLES

Sometimes the court could find no convenient rule in its various sources to support what it wanted to do, or there appeared in its sources a rule that ran contrary to what it wanted to do. In such cases it was always open to the court to relapse into the disciplinary mode and act outside and apart from any rules, according to disciplinary principles, however arbitrary the results might appear to be.

Two such principles are worthy of mention here as being characteristic features of disciplinary systems. These are, on the criminal side, the principle of punishing any conduct at all which in the view of the court amounts to conduct to the prejudice of good order, or which for any other reason in the view of the court calls for suppression, and on the civil side, the principle of deciding disputes, not according to rigid imperatives and the strict rights of individuals, but according to all the circumstances of the particular case, having regard to the interests of the group. In this latter mode any rules that may apply are not treated as determinative imperatives but only as part of the surrounding circumstances to be looked at.

PUNISHMENT FOR DOING WHAT OUGHT NOT TO BE DONE

Thus, for an example on the criminal side, there was a section in the Provisional Criminal Code, Article 10, which provided that "No act constitutes an offense unless the same is specifically made so by law." This did not deter the Mixed Court from frequently convicting and punishing Chinese for the offense of "returning to the Settlement after expulsion," although such an offense was quite unknown to anything that could be called "law" within the meaning of Article 10. The Mixed Court regularly ordered the expulsion of undesirables from the settlement. This was done sometimes as an addition to a punishment for a criminal offense, sometimes apart from any criminal offense upon a charge (for which there was no legal authority) of "being an undesirable and a menace to the peace and order of the Settlement," and sometimes without any charge at all being brought. In these cases, of course, the Mixed Court was not acting as a legal tribunal at all, but as a group-disciplinary tribunal, punishing on behalf of the leaders of the group disobedience to orders and insubordination, and imposing upon unwanted group members, at will, the familiar sanction in group disciplinary societies of expulsion from the group.

The lack of any legal basis for these procedures was emphasized by the Chinese when in February 1914 the British assessor in the International Settlement requested the authorities in the Chinese city to cooperate in making these expulsions effective. The Chinese refused on the ground that since the promulgation of the Provisional Criminal Code such procedures were no longer permissible.[60] The Provisional Court of Jiangsu, when it took over the work of the Mixed Court in January 1927, proclaimed in one of its earliest judgments that the practices of expelling undesirables from the settlement and punishing those who returned after expulsion were illegal and that the court in future would not be a party to any such action.[61]

In the case of *Mun. Police v. King and anr.* the charge was "conspiring with others with intent to promote litigation in the Mixed Court." The essence of the conduct complained of was "touting" for business. Counsel for the defense argued vigorously and persuasively that no such offense was known in China, neither in the traditional system nor in the modern code. In view of Article 10, he argued, the Mixed Court could not create an offense where there was none. The assessor said that the question was whether the court would take cognizance of the facts of the case as an offense. The magistrate and he had decided that in order to uphold the dignity of the court it must be an offense. He explained further that there were many gaps in the Provisional Criminal Code. There was, he said, "no offence in Chinese law of holding oneself out to be a lawyer when in fact one is not, but it was constituted an offence for the reason that the public had to be protected from persons of the very type of the accused." The court convicted and sentenced the accused.[62] In this case the court was again acting in the disciplinary and not in the adjudicative mode. In disciplinary systems it is competent for a tribunal to punish, and expected of it that it will punish any conduct which it thinks deserves suppression, whether such conduct has been specifically prohibited in any predetermined rule or not. In military systems the charge is framed as "conduct to the prejudice of good order and military discipline." In the disciplinary system of traditional China the offense was simply "doing what ought not to be done."[63]

Similarly, in civil proceedings the court was prepared, when occasion demanded, to depart from settled rules and legal principles recognized in the West and decide an issue according to what it thought best in all the circumstances of the particular case and in the interests of the group.

Sometimes the court's flexibility in this respect was presented starkly without any attempt at disguise, and in such cases the result might appear to a Western lawyer's mind remarkable, if not bizarre. Thus in the case of *Vinogradoff v. China Merchants Steam Navigation Co.* the plaintiff suffered an injury by a fall from a ladder on the ship where he was employed as second officer, and became permanently disabled from following his profession as a ship's officer. He alleged the ladder was unsafe and sued the shipowners in negligence. The court found that the defendant company was entirely free from any blame, that the plaintiff's fall was partly due to his own carelessness and that the plaintiff's permanent disability was due to venereal disease. The court thereupon entered judgment for the plaintiff with heavy damages and costs.[64] The defendants, regarding the amount awarded as excessive, sought through consular intervention a review of the judgment, but one limited only to the amount of damages awarded.[65]

It may be borne in mind in considering this judgment that according to traditional Chinese group-disciplinary attitudes to dispute resolution in cases where compensation for damage or injury was claimed, the question of which party was richer and better able to pay for the damage was often regarded as more relevant and more directly determinative than the question of which party was negligent.[66]

It should also be noticed that in Western seafaring tradition there is a general principle of very ancient origin, dating from before the laws of Oleron and Wisby, to the effect that a ship owner owes a special duty of care to any sailors who fall sick or suffer injury during a voyage from any cause, whether due to the owner's fault or not. Broadly the owner is expected to maintain a sick crew member, to pay wages, and to meet medical expenses until the sailor can be put ashore at the home port.

In Great Britain these traditions were given statutory expression in a precise and more modern form in the Merchant Shipping Acts dating from 1854. In the United States of America the sailor's right is known as the right to "maintenance and cure." In 1903 Mr. Justice Brown defined it thus: "That the vessel and her owners are liable in case a seaman falls sick or is wounded in the service of the ship to the extent of his maintenance and cure and to his wages at least so long as the voyage is continued."[67] In 1949 Mr. Justice Jackson, speaking of the plaintiff seaman in *Farrell v. United States,* said, "His fall was due to no negligence but his own," and held him entitled to "the usual measure of maintenance and cure at the ship's expense."[68]

None of these considerations, of course, impose any legal liability upon a Chinese ship owner in China. Nor are they directly relevant even by analogy where, as in this case, the voyage was over and the seaman's claim was based on the owner's negligence. However, there was a scale of compensation recognized in Shanghai according to which the shipping companies, both Chinese and foreign, were accustomed to pay their employees who suffered injury. This modest compensation the defendant in this case had always been ready to pay.

Perhaps the judgment may be rationalized in terms of Western thought as meaning that the court absolved the ship owner of any culpability but found that, according to "general legal principles" observed among seafaring nations, a ship owner was always under some special degree of liability to care for a sailor injured in the owner's employ, and in assessing this liability the court found that the man's need was great and that the defendant could afford to pay a substantial sum in excess of the scale figure. But this is only an artificial rationalization designed to make the decision more acceptable in a Western lawyer's mind. It does not necessarily represent in any way what the court actually thought or felt about the matter.

Sometimes the Mixed Court presented its flexibility and freedom from the restraints of inexorable imperatives in a more subtle way than in Vinogradoff's case. Thus Grant Jones, British assessor, in *International Export Co. v. Hope Bros. and Wood*[69] found that there was a well-established rule in England that a foreign instrument which is negotiable in its country of origin is not a negotiable instrument in England so as to give a bona fide holder for value good title against the true owner of the instrument from whom it had been stolen. Here then was a well-recognized legal principle upon which Grant Jones might have been expected to found his judgment. But it did not give him the result he wanted. He saw that if he applied this rule in conditions of extraterritoriality then the same check would be a negotiable instrument in the British consular and supreme courts but a nonnegotiable instrument in the Mixed Court. He did not want that, so he simply rejected the established principle and declared the check a negotiable instrument in the Mixed Court. But he did not do this baldly as I have stated it. He did it in the language and idiom of the English common-law system of jurisprudence. He adopted the stance of a court of appeal engaged in a piece of judicial law-making by rejecting an existing line of precedent and starting a new line with a new precedent. He rejected the established rule as unsuitable for conditions of extraterritoriality and purported to substitute a new principle especially evolved and enunciated by himself for the purpose. He said:

> The principle which we must I think, lay down is this: that natives of this country dealing with a foreign instrument do so subject to all the incidents which attach to it in the country of its origin, and every such instrument is prima facie to be construed and governed by the law and custom in which it has its source.

In reality of course Grant Jones was not "laying down" any principle or line of authority at all. He was altering no imperatives and setting no new ones. The Mixed Court was no superior court of appeal. It had no means of establishing or enforcing any doctrine of *stare decisis*. There was no compelling reason why any court, even the Mixed Court itself, should follow Grant Jones and accept as an invariable rule the principle he "laid down." He was in fact doing nothing more and could do nothing more than to decide the case before him. In so doing he was having regard first to group convenience and coherence rather than to well-settled rules. Thus he resolved the issue for this case only, in the way that he thought would best make for harmony and consistency in the decisions of the discordant variety of national courts in the settlement and in the best interests of the groups. He was being as arbitrary as the court was in the Vinogradoff case but he presented his arbitrary decision so that it seemed to accord better with the principles of an adjudicative system.

In another case, H. Bucknell, the American assessor, in 1926 was quite prepared to act outside accepted legal principles of the immunity of sovereign states and to give judgment against a Soviet Government shipping line by way of relief against a trading liability. In the sequel the defendant was able to bring the matter up again for rehearing by way of appeal before the Provisional Court of Jiangsu. In the provisional court, Dr. John C. H. Wu reasserted the supremacy of transcendent rigid rules over the shifting standards of group disciplinary expediency and reversed Bucknell's judgment.[70]

Sometimes the Mixed Court was prepared to acknowledge openly its flexibility and freedom to act as it chose. In the case of *Chang Shih-chao v. Wu Ting-fang*, the British assessor, Blackburn, addressing counsel for the defense, who was American, said:

> If we were to allow ourselves to be tied down strictly by the rules of procedure and of law known in your country and mine we should probably not be able to make any progress whatsoever in this case. . . . We are quite prepared to admit that [in granting an injunction] we have not been guided by any legal principles or any rule of law—the only principle by which we have been guided is that of holding the scales as evenly as possible between the parties.[71]

The court's flexibility and freedom to please itself were not limited to individual cases but sometimes were exercised, as it were, by wholesale.

In 1918 a code of "Rules for the Application of Foreign Laws" was promulgated by mandate issued from Beijing. This decreed that in respect of foreign nationals without benefit of extraterritoriality, civil rights and obligations arising between themselves should, in certain specified fields, be governed by "the national law of the parties." The Mixed Court pleased itself how far it would obey this rule. In cases between German nationals it was content to ignore it.[72] In cases between Russian nationals it was persuaded to honor the rule, at least selectively.[73] Furthermore, the court decided for itself which types of cases it would accept and which it would not. Until 1924 it refused to hear Russian divorce cases, but after that date it relented and began to accept them.[74]

The court's potential for flexibility in judgment was further enhanced by the lack of any provision for appeal. It was not impossible sometimes to persuade the court to reverse itself on rehearing but there was no superior court of appeal to lay down guidelines and ensure that the court kept within them.

There was consequently no enforceable principle of *stare decisis*. The court was of course not unaware of the value to litigants of consistency in its judgments.[75] At the same time, in disciplinary fashion, it was not prepared to hamper its freedom of movement on any given occasion by anything it might have done previously. Its position in this respect was expressed in the following extract from the registrar's report for January 1924:

> On several occasions on the hearing of Chinese civil actions lawyers in their arguments referred to court decisions and orders rendered prior to the case at issue and tried to insist that these earlier decisions must be upheld. In one case the Bench found it necessary to point out that such earlier decisions might hamper the exercise of justice and that consequently the court was in no way bound to look upon earlier decisions as precedents. It would only take into consideration the facts of each particular case and would be guided by law and equity.[76]

CHINESE DIRECTION OF THE COURT REJECTED

The assessors, in pursuance of their attempt to lead the Mixed Court out of the disciplinary and into the adjudicative mode of the maintenance of order, were always zealous to proclaim the complete independence of the court from subordination to direction or influence of any kind. The Chinese, for their part, never wavered in their attitude that the court must take direction, like any other instrumentality in a disciplinary society, from higher authority, and during the period 1911 to 1927 they made frequent attempts to exercise a power of direction over the Mixed Court.

Thus in 1917 when China declared war on Germany and Austria-Hungary, the commissioner for foreign affairs for Jiangsu wrote to the Mixed Court magistrate instructing him that he was not to extend any leniency to any Austrians who might come before him, Austrians having now lost their extraterritorial rights. The commissioner added: "The [Mixed] Court is subject to the control of this office and its affairs are to be administered under my directions. You will be so good as to act in accordance with my instructions."[77]

The assessors, however, would not permit any direction of the court by Chinese authority. They vigorously rejected and frustrated all such attempts whenever they became aware of any. Thus in 1919 in the case of *Passeri v. The Bureau of Liquidation,* the magistrate, Yui, in giving a judgment dissenting from that of the assessor, admitted that strong representations had been made to him by the commissioner for foreign affairs on behalf of the Beijing Government and that he could not ignore those representations. It was clear that he had dissented from the assessor in accordance with instructions received.[78]

In 1924, in *Municipal Police v. four men,* the assessor complained that a criminal attempt had been made by the Chinese Chamber of Commerce to interfere with the administration of justice in the case, and that similar attempts had been made by the chamber to influence the decision of the court in civil cases, by making representations to the magistrate. He said that the practice appeared to be tolerated by certain Chinese courts in spite of the theoretically independent status of the modern courts in China and that he would take no action at present but would view seriously any continuance of such attempts.[79]

CONSULAR DIRECTION OF THE COURT

In June 1917 a Turkish citizen in the employ of the German consulate and suspected of being a German spy was brought before Magistrate Waung and British Assessor Grant Jones for trial. Defending counsel, an Austrian, argued that Grant Jones, as a British consular officer, must necessarily be prejudiced, Britain then being at war with Germany, Turkey, and Austria. Grant Jones disagreed. "I sit here to do justice," he declared somewhat grandly, "and while in this court I accept no dictation from my authorities."[80]

But in spite of these brave words and in spite of the assessors' insistence on the court's independence and their vigorous rejection of any attempt by the Chinese to direct it, their attitude toward consular direction was in fact rather different. In practice the court never failed to respect and to act upon the directives of the consuls, if and when the consuls saw fit to issue any. Given the group-disciplinary nature of the International Settlement and its control mechanisms, matters could hardly be otherwise. The court was constituted by the mere fiat of the consuls as group leaders, and its jurisdiction was delimited by consular directives. The only warrant for the presence of the foreign assessor on the bench in purely Chinese cases was the direction of the consuls to the court that it should be so. The rules of procedure for such cases rested in nothing more than the edict of the consuls. The assessors were not independent but were junior consular officers responsible to their consuls-general and bound to accept directions if and when their superiors saw fit to give any. The magistrates had no security of tenure. They were appointed by the consuls and occupied their offices at the consuls' pleasure.

Nevertheless, owing to the consuls' restraint, the court was, in practice, able to enjoy a high degree of independence. The consuls only interfered, as a rule, in matters which involved political questions of an international nature, matters of consular policy, and cases where consular direction was specifically asked for by the court. Thus, in 1912 in a case where there were political overtones and questions of public safety involved, the court adjourned in order to consult the consular body. On resumption the court found the accused guilty and imposed a fine of four hundred dollars. When challenged by defending counsel to say whether this judgment was the judgment of the court, the assessor replied "it is announced by this court on the advice of the Consular Body."[81]

In 1926, in *Consul-General for the Netherlands v. Weidemann,* the court was asked by the Netherlands police to extradite to Surabaja a German national accused of committing a crime in Java, then a Netherlands dependency. Counsel opposing the application took the point that rights to extradition were grounded solely in treaty, and that in the case of the Netherlands-China treaties, extradition was limited to Netherlands citizens. Extradition of a German citizen was not provided for. This was a plain legal point for the decision of the court in the ordinary course, but the court decided to refer it first to the consular body for an opinion. Counsel for the defense, with the ready permission of the court, submitted his arguments in writing to the consular body direct. The consular body gave an opinion favorable to the accused and the application for extradition was dismissed.[82]

In October 1913 a claim was brought in the Mixed Court against a Chinese family for repayment of a debt of over half a million taels, and in default for sale of the undivided joint family property which had been mortgaged to secure the loan. No defense was offered on the merits, but an objection to the jurisdiction was raised on the ground that two members of the family had acquired Japanese nationality and two members Portuguese nationality, and consequently could not be sued in the Mixed Court but only in the courts of their own consuls. The court, Magistrate Guan, and British Assessor Grant Jones, held that the action was not taken against the Japanese and Portuguese nationals individually, but against a Chinese undivided family organization. They overruled the objection to the jurisdiction, gave judgment for the plaintiffs, and ordered a sale of the property.[83] The Japanese and Portuguese consuls took objection to this judgment and complained to the British consul-general, who ordered the British assessor to suspend the judgment and not to allow its enforcement. The British assessor had no option but to obey his instructions. This had the effect of negating the Mixed Court proceedings and nullifying its judgment entirely. Fortunately for the judgment creditors, the trustees of the land were British citizens, and it proved possible therefore to apply to His Britannic Majesty's Supreme Court for China for authority to sell the land. There,

Mr. Justice Bourne expressed entire approval of the judgment of the Mixed Court and gave a decision in the British court to the same effect, ordering the sale of the land. The judge said: "I do not understand the meaning of the suspension of the Mixed Court judgment. I don't see how the judgment itself could be suspended. The judgment can only be set aside by a court of appeal."[84]

A leader in the *North China Herald* echoed the judge's remarks with praise and approval.[85] The judge and the leader-writer were, of course, thinking and writing in terms of Western jurisprudence. If they had been accustomed to think and feel in terms of disciplinary theory, they would have realized at once that they were in the presence of one of the characteristic features that identify a disciplinary system: there is no objection or difficulty at all in such a system about a nonjudicial authority reviewing, suspending, or reversing the judgment of a disciplinary tribunal. Indeed it is the regular and proper practice in such systems.

It is not suggested that the consuls stepped in very often in this fashion, but the case is noteworthy as an indication of how far the consuls could go if they had a mind to. Most of the time they had no need to be so obvious. Thus on 5 November 1912 the senior consul wrote to the senior magistrate, Guan Jiong, advising him that the consular body took the view that the sentence of twenty years imprisonment imposed on one Wan Fu-hua in 1904 was too severe and the court was invited to reconsider the case in a spirit of clemency with a view to remitting or mitigating the former sentence. The senior consul added that any remission of the prisoner's term of confinement would have to be accompanied by an order for his perpetual expulsion from the settlement. On 7 December 1912 the Mixed Court ordered the immediate release of the prisoner and ordered that he be expelled from the settlement never to return.[86]

Throughout the whole period 1911 to 1927, the consuls' control of the court was much more than merely constitutional and administrative. In one of the very first cases heard in the Mixed Court after the consular takeover in 1911, counsel for the municipal police, prosecuting, asked for a penalty of imprisonment. The assessor remanded the prisoners and, on resumption, said, "The senior consul thinks that a fine is adequate," and a fine was imposed accordingly.[87] In one of the very last important cases heard in the Mixed Court before its abolition at the end of 1926, the British consul-general instructed the assessor as to the attitude and the view he was to adopt in the case and what he should do if the magistrate differed from him.[88]

SUMMARY OF PRINCIPLES GUIDING THE MIXED COURT

Formulating now the major principles upon which the Mixed Court was accustomed to act in coming to its decisions, we arrive at the following broad conclusions. First, the court obeyed consular directives and followed consular indications whenever any were given. Second, the court resisted and rejected Chinese directives and influence whenever an attempt was made to extend any. Third, subject to consular direction and consular policy, the court preserved complete flexibility and freedom to act in each case as it saw fit. It recognized no binding force in precedent and no principle of *stare decisis*.

Fourth, the court did not operate in the presence of any corpus of universal, predetermined, transcendent imperatives of conduct, such as are the sine qua non of the adjudicative concept. Where there existed established and recognized rules, the court was able very largely to pick and choose which rules or sets of rules it would observe and accept for enforcement and which it would ignore.

Fifth, although in the last resort the court was not necessarily bound by any rules, nevertheless in practice it followed rules almost, although not quite, all of the time. In municipal matters it enforced, and followed quite strictly, the land regulations and the byelaws and ordinances of the municipal council. In its criminal administration it followed closely, but with some exceptions, the Provisional Criminal Code. In civil matters it brought itself under appropriate written mandates, orders, and regulations, when it could find ones that suited its purpose. When it could not, it invoked well-settled principles of Chinese custom and Western jurisprudence, which it could call principles of universal application or at least general acceptance.

In this way the court was able most of the time to escape the stigma of arbitrariness, and to claim that it acted according to predetermined imperatives in the adjudicative mode. The assessors, or at least the British and American assessors, strove honestly and conscientiously to wean the Chinese magistrates away from the disciplinary mode and to introduce the principles of the adjudicative mode and of judicial independence. In pursuing these objectives they succeeded most of the time in making the proceedings of the court look very like the proceedings of an adjudicative tribunal, but they were hampered by the absence of the basic requirement of the adjudicative concept, a comprehensive and coherent system of inexorable imperatives to administer. To supply this deficiency they claimed from time to time that the court was bound by and administering "Chinese law." We have found, however, on examination that the expression "Chinese law" did not denote any coherent identifiable system of transcendent and universal imperatives and can only be regarded as a piece of backward translation. It is no more than an instance of the projection of the images of Western jurisprudence upon the realities of the Chinese disciplinary system, distorting and caricaturing them beyond recognition.

In the end it became clear that the battle the assessors were fighting in the Mixed Court was not, after all, as they imagined, a struggle to oust the disciplinary mode and to replace it with the adjudicative. The contest remained what it had always been since the Mixed Court first opened its doors in 1864—a contest to decide whether the consuls or the Chinese should be the superior authority to direct and to instruct the court as it continued unwaveringly to operate in the disciplinary mode.

The Mixed Court was and remained to the end a creature of the society of contending groups into which it was born—itself a prisoner of the group-disciplinary system, tied inescapably to the principles of disciplinary theory. It carried with it to its demise in 1926 the badge of its parenthood.

CHAPTER 7

Assessment of the Work of the Mixed Court 1911–27

More than sixty years having elapsed since the Mixed Court of the International Settlement at Shanghai was abolished, it is now possible to attempt with the advantage that this historical perspective affords some critical assessment of the work of the court from 1911 to 1927. The court has not attracted that degree of scholarly attention and comment that the interest of its constitution and the implications of its work would seem to deserve.

Mark Elvin is responsible for the best and most authoritative modern study of the Mixed Court in depth. He offers a short but scholarly and perceptive assessment of the place and the work of the Mixed Court, in its relation particularly to the social history of the International Settlement, up to 1911. Unfortunately he does not deal with the court at all after the consuls took it over in 1911.[1]

Norwood F. Allman published in 1924 a short assessment of the work of the Mixed Court entitled "What the Shanghai Mixed Court Is and What It Does." Allman was at that time practicing before the court and had previously served as American assessor on the bench of the court. The article was, however, written for a popular weekly and not for a learned journal and is far too short to do much more than touch upon the major highlights. It was designed to correct some of the uninformed misconceptions then current in Shanghai about the court.[2]

Randall T. Bell, in an illuminating study, has compared the Courts of the Staple in England in the fourteenth century with the Mixed Court of Shanghai in the nineteenth and early twentieth centuries and has explored the remarkable similarities and common characteristics that exist between them.[3] His study, however, does not attempt any comprehensive coverage of the Mixed Court nor assessment of its achievements. Apart from these writers, assessment of the work of the Mixed Court has been generally inadequate and unsatisfying.

Anatol M. Kotenev must, of course, be given credit for his industry in compiling his manual on the history and practice of the Mixed Court, but his evaluations of the thrust and significance of its work were erratic and cannot, unfortunately, be accepted without question. Kotenev was a Russian refugee, physically disabled, and owed his livelihood to his employment by the municipal council. This close involvement with the council and his loyalty to his employer clouded his judgment. He was neither distanced nor disinterested enough for the task of objective assessment.

In his first book, *Shanghai: Its Mixed Court and Council*, published in April 1925, he is full of enthusiasm for the success of the International Settlement, the municipal council, and the Mixed Court.[4] He declared that the intervention of modern European jurists in the persons of the foreign assessors had transformed the Mixed Court into a unique institution which succeeded "in reconciling the conflicting principles of the European and Chinese psychologies and establishing workable machinery for the administration of justice."[5] This of course is exactly what the court did *not* succeed in doing, and he himself soon came to realize how wrong he had been. He published his second book, *Shanghai: Its Municipality and the Chinese*, in March 1927. In the meantime Shanghai had been hit by the tragic antiforeign riots of May 1925 and by the calamitous antiforeign strikes and boycotts of the later months of that year, the Mixed Court itself had been abolished, and its place had been taken by a court under Chinese control. The confidence and complacency of the foreign element in Shanghai had been badly shaken. Kotenev is now on the defensive; he is much more subdued and there can be detected even a note of shock and dismay.

He does however discuss the Ming Sung Umbrella case at some length.[6] This was a case where the Chinese magistrate and the British assessor failed to agree; their conflicting attitudes could not be reconciled, and an impasse in the administration of dispute resolution ensued. Kotenev treats this case on the basis that the "organic differences in the foreign and Chinese psychologies" had *not* been reconciled, that they remained as divisive as ever, that they were closely reflected in the Ming Sung Umbrella hearing, and that the arguments in that case "revealed once more the complete divergency of the opinions of foreigners and Chinese on the construction of law." He takes the view that no decision was possible in the Ming Sung Umbrella case that could have satisfied both parties, since the mutual divergencies were not reconcilable. He declares that the foreigners must now either recognize Chinese nationalism, give up extraterritoriality, and accept Chinese tradition, or else denounce utterly the Chinese ideology and compel China to accept Western principles. He concludes with a curt *tertium non datur* (no third course is open). This result is exactly the reverse of his previous assessment that the court had succeeded in reconciling Chinese psychology with Western jurisprudence, and had established "workable machinery" for the administration of justice.

Kotenev's works, in spite of his prolix and somewhat turgid style, still offer valuable source material of fact and record, and they could have been, as he intended them, useful handbooks for legal practitioners and businessmen in Shanghai if the Mixed Court had survived long enough to sustain a need for them. But it is necessary for the historian to be wary of Kotenev's appreciations, interpretations, and evaluations of the significance of the facts and occurrences that he lived so close to and that affected him so nearly.

In 1927 Manley O. Hudson, Professor of International Law at Harvard, included a brief sketch of the Mixed Court and its history in an article on the circumstances of its rendition to Chinese authority.[7] His treatment in this article is, however, factual rather than analytical. He ventures little upon interpretation. He summarizes the performance of the Mixed Court before 1911 with a cautious, "It may be doubted whether the Mixed Court was at any time during this period a satisfactory tribunal."[8] He offers no assessment of the court's performance after 1911.

Unfortunately, but very naturally of course, this distinguished scholar looked at the Mixed Court only through the spectacles of a Western expert in international law. He found the community the court served "curious,"[9] and its "administration of justice" "peculiar,"[10] and he left it at that. With great respect to Hudson one may ask, Could it be that his article demonstrates for all to see how inadequate and indeed how irrelevant the concepts and approaches of international law are found to be in the interpretation of a disciplinary situation?

Johnstone in 1936 gave the Mixed Court a factual and dispassionate, if somewhat pedestrian, treatment of twenty-five pages covering the court's entire lifespan from 1864 to 1927.[11] This is a careful and scholarly sketch but must, of course, in view of its shortness be very general. He does not attempt any analysis in depth and does not contribute anything significant to an understanding of the Mixed Court experience in its deeper implications. Since then few sinologists have devoted to the Mixed Court any more attention than a slight (and often slighting and ill-informed) reference in passing. No one has attempted a balanced and objective assessment of its achievements or a considered interpretation of its more profound implications.

THE COURT'S PRIMARY ROLE

The primary function of the Mixed Court was to support the consuls, the municipal council, and the muncipal police in the repression of crime, the maintenance of good order, and the enforcement of the council ordinances among the Chinese within the settlement. It will be noted that this primary function has been defined, as is appropriate to a group-disciplinary community, in terms of disciplinary theory, not in terms of Western legal theory. We have not said that the court's primary function was to administer impartially without fear or favor the rules of a criminal code or of any other kind of a behavioral code of transcendent imperatives. Still less have we said that the court's function was to "dispense justice," whatever that cant phrase may mean.

The court performed very well its primary function as we have described it. Its hearings were prompt, summary, and decisive. There were no preliminary committal proceedings and no jury trials to delay swift retribution for wrongdoing. The court rarely allowed argument over technical matters such as the admission of evidence, questions of jurisdiction, or questions of the construction of a rule, to delay a decision for long. It maintained at all times good relations with the consuls, the municipal council, and the police. In accordance with the principles of disciplinary systems the court never failed to conform with consular directives and to respond favorably to any indications of consular policy or consular desires. So also, in support of the municipal council, the court, acting in the disciplinary mode, never failed to give effect to municipal ordinances however much the council's authority, in a legal sense, to issue them might be questioned or questionable. As for the police, the court was not slow to commend police publicly for their diligence and courage whenever circumstances warranted it. The police seldom had any occasion to complain about the support afforded them by the court.

The significance for Shanghai of the court's effective discharge of its primary function was reflected in the success of consular and municipal control of conditions within the International Settlement. Backed by the Mixed Court, the municipal council was able to maintain, in a population that was 90 percent Chinese, a much higher standard of security, orderliness, cleanliness, and health than was to be found outside settlement limits. In May 1926 on the occasion of the inauguration by Sun Chuanfang of his concept of "Greater Shanghai"—a municipal organization for the Chinese city outside the settlement—he made a speech in which he referred to his idea of gradually converting the area outside the foreign settlements into a model city, the result of which should form the basis for our demand for the abolishing of foreign concessions. This has been one of my dearest dreams, for whenever I come to a treaty port I feel thoroughly humiliated, not only because a treaty port is a standing reminder of our loss of sovereignty, but also because whenever we pass from the concessions into Chinese territory we feel that we are crossing into a different world—the former is the upper and the latter is the underworld, for nothing in the Chinese territory—roads, buildings, or public health—can be compared with the concessions. This is the greatest of our national humiliations, much greater in my opinion than the loss of sovereignty.[12]

Conditions within the settlement and council control of municipal affairs had previously been the subject on more than one occasion of admiration, emulation, and conscious imitation by Chinese authorities outside the settlement.[13] In view of its limited legal authority under the land regulations, the municipal council could never have attained this result without the support of the Mixed Court in upholding, disciplinary fashion, the council's own ordinances.

THE SECOND ROLE OF THE MIXED COURT

The second role of the Mixed Court was to support the consuls, the council, the police, and the Shanghai Volunteer Corps in their policy of protecting Chinese residents of the settlement from the arbitrary forfeiture of their lives and property at the hands of their fellow Chinese outside the settlement. This necessity first came into prominence in the 1850s when the settlement was flooded with Chinese refugees seeking safety and protection from the rapine and slaughter of the Taiping civil wars.

In the period 1911–27 the court afforded Chinese residents protection from exploitation and personal violence at the hands of Chinese outside the settlement chiefly in four ways. First the court refused to recognize the validity or force of any attempt by any authority outside the settlement to levy, however lawfully, any taxation upon any person within the settlement except such as might be approved by the settlement group-leaders—the consuls and the municipal council. It had been acknowledged since very early in the history of the settlement that according to Western legal principles the Chinese sovereign government had every right to tax Chinese nationals in the settlement. But, following characteristically group-disciplinary procedures, the leaders of the group retained and exercised the power to refuse recognition within the group to the taxation levies of political powers outside the group.[14]

In the course of time this denial of sovereign taxation rights came to be defended in legal terminology as a long-established usage. Enforced by the Mixed Court this policy ensured that the wealth and property of Chinese within the settlement remained protected against the savage exploitation by taxing authorities that commonly occurred outside the settlement.

Second, the court punished severely any attempt at illegal extortion by force or threats that might occur within the settlement and come to its notice. Outside the settlement, "squeeze" and extortion were part of the everyday burden that trade was regularly called upon to bear.

Third, the court, following consular policy and long-established practice, insisted that no Chinese within the settlement might be taken into custody by, or handed over to, officers of any outside authority unless there had been established against him in open court a prima-facie case of the commission of a criminal offense. This meant the commission by him of some act that the Mixed Court was prepared to recognize as criminal and did not regard as merely an act of political deviance or dissidence. This procedure also involved a denial of the sovereign power of the Chinese government to control and dispose of its own citizens on its own soil. It could not be justified on any legal ground unless upon the plea of long-established usage.

Fourth, the court exercised the consuls' extralegal power, as group-leaders, of expelling from the community as undesirables those who extorted money or tried to enforce without consular sanction the orders, claims, or demands upon a resident of any authority outside the settlement.

This protection of Chinese nationals, the second role of the Mixed Court, it carried out with firmness, decision, and success. Throughout all the political vicissitudes of the Yuan Shikai era and the decline and extinguishment of any central government in China, throughout all the marching and countermarching of the armies of the warlords and their murdering and marauding hordes, the Mixed Court carried out the consuls' policy of protection of resident Chinese and their business and property, unruffled and undisturbed. Throughout the stresses and strains occasioned in the largely European international community of the settlement by the European war of 1914–18 and the loss of extraterritorial rights by Germans, Austrians, and Russians, the court never faltered.

The court's ability to rise above and survive unscathed the catastrophic upheavals in China and Europe of the period 1911–27 was very much assisted by the circumstance that it was not the creature of any sovereign national power and not bound up with the fate of any. It was very careful not to allow itself to become involved in the quarrels of the warring nations and factions. Its existence, its allegiance, and its duty were cognizable and comprehensible only in terms of group-disciplinary systems. It owed loyalty only to the group which it served, and without which it had no meaning, the group-community of the International Settlement.

The significance for the International Settlement of the court's performance in its second role was incalculable. It is reflected in the circumstance that, in Eric Teichman's words, "Shanghai remained an oasis of peace, order and good government, in a China torn into convulsions by revolution, banditry and civil war."[15] The settlement remained one of the few spots in China where wealthy Chinese, even defeated warlords and successful merchants, could reside with their families and property in a high degree of personal safety. It was a place where they could carry on their business affairs unhindered, with a reasonable prospect of retaining their profits, or most of their profits, for themselves. It is true that this security was only one of the factors which accounted for the dramatic development of trade and prosperity in Shanghai over the period 1911–27. It was however a sine qua non. It is safe to say that without the cooperation and loyal support of the Mixed Court, their order-enforcement tribunal, the consuls and the council could never have ensured to Chinese businessmen and Chinese interests that degree of reliable security upon the basis of which it was possible to develop Shanghai into the largest and most prosperous city in China and the fifth largest port in the world.

THE THIRD ROLE OF THE MIXED COURT

The third function of the Mixed Court was to determine disputes in all cases where Chinese, or foreigners without treaty rights, were defendants. It assumed this function both in mixed cases, that is where the plaintiff was a foreigner, and in purely Chinese cases, that is where the plaintiff as well as the defendant was Chinese. Again the court performed its role very creditably.

It strove to introduce, so far as it could, Western standards of impartiality, honesty, and integrity into dispute resolution. No moral judgments are being suggested here. We are not in the slightest concerned with the question of which were morally more righteous, the Chinese or the Western standards of impartiality, honesty, and integrity. All that is being suggested is that in a context of trade, Western standards in these matters lent a much greater degree of predictability and certainty, and therefore of profitability, to the outcome of commercial transactions and disputes than did the Chinese standards, by letting it be known beforehand that disputes were to be resolved according to predetermined and fixed rules, and not according to unpredictable and uncontrollable edicts of men.

The court aimed at eliminating the determinative influence of the guilds and chambers of commerce in civil disputes. We are not concerned with whether this was or was not a praiseworthy objective according to any absolute or nationalistic or societal standards or ideals. We are only concerned to point out that it was praiseworthy in the sense of its encouragement of trade and commerce in the development of Shanghai. The court did not in practice always achieve the standard in these matters of impartiality, integrity, and honesty that the British and American assessors aimed at, but the ideals were always there and were persistently striven for.

In their devotion to this ideal of dispute resolution according to predetermined, known, and rigid standards, the assessors were continually engaged in an unending struggle to construct and define a corpus or framework of fixed universal rules according to which they might give judgment in the style of the adjudicative mode of Western jurisprudence. In another improvement, the court no longer relied, as previously, merely upon the arrest and detention of debtors to enforce payment of a judgment debt. It now introduced measures for the enforcement of its judgments by seizure and sale of the debtor's property and by bankruptcy administration. This ensured much more prompt and effective execution of its judgments and thereby remedied one of the chief complaints laid at the door of the Mixed Court as it operated before 1911.

The assessors ensured that the court gave a hearing as of right to every petition for redress of a civil wrong that was presented. Under the traditional Chinese system no one had any right to have his plaint heard, but the magistrate was able to, and did, arbitrarily reject petitions without investigation, and those which he did condescend to investigate were accepted for hearing purely as a matter of grace. The court put an end to this system and ensured that every bona fide complaint should be heard.

The significance of these reforms and changes, and of the better performance by the court of its third role, dispute resolution, lay particularly in the encouragement, security, and stimulus that they gave to trade. Merchants are able to commit much larger sums to much expanded commercial activities when they know that their contracts will be enforced according to their terms and to known rules, not according to the whim of some guild officers or some irresponsible mediator acting at large. This kind of relative certainty of outcome goes a long way toward making it possible for large modern corporations such as banks, insurance companies, and steamship lines to exist and flourish. Western experience shows that it is not necessary that many cases should actually go to court, so long as there is a court standing by, accessible to traders, which can and does enforce its decisions, and so long as the principles and rules that the court will apply are in general predetermined, known, and constant. The Mixed Court was able to come much closer to fulfilling these requirements than any tribunal under the traditional Chinese systems could possibly come.

There were of course security devices built into indigenous Chinese trading practices. A very common device was the joinder of guarantors, men of substance who could not afford the loss of face that default would incur, and of these the Western traders made regular and consistent use. Nevertheless it may be affirmed that the expansion and development of modern trade between Western and Chinese interests that took place in Shanghai could not have reached the heights they did in the absence of the regulating and facilitating influence of some such dispute resolution tribunal as the Mixed Court.

This is not to say that the Chinese were quick to welcome and embrace the Western system. They were not. Chinese political authorities and business group leaders felt keenly the restraints upon their traditional paramount command over hierarchical inferiors. In particular they bitterly resented the refusal of the Mixed Court to take orders and directions from them and did all they could to resist the Western influence and reestablish the old system of their domination over the court.

THE LESSER ROLES OF THE MIXED COURT

The court also fulfilled a number of lesser roles. These were all related directly to the orderliness and convenience of the international settlement as a place for merchants to live, and to the provision of facilities ancillary to carrying on trade. First, the court undertook coroner's inquests where the deceased was a Chinese national or an unprotected foreigner. Second, it exercised for the consuls their function, as leaders of the community, of expelling from the settlement persons who were deemed a threat to the peace and order or to the cohesion of the community or who were otherwise classifiable as undesirables. This was a procedure in the disciplinary not the adjudicative mode, being the exercise of one of the characteristic features of group-disciplinary systems, the summary expulsion from the group of members posing a threat to the cohesion and survival of the group. Third, the court exercised the supreme prerogative of mercy, releasing prisoners from jail, sometimes upon the representations of the consuls and sometimes upon the declaration of an amnesty by the Chinese government. Fourth, the court performed the function of a deeds registration office, or office of records. It accepted deeds and documents of all kinds, or copies of them, for record, and at the request of the parties it registered them and filed them away for production again whenever required for evidence or for examination. Fifth, the court undertook bankruptcy administrations and liquidations for business associations, the work of winding-up being done by a European firm of official accountants and receivers appointed by the court, answering only to the court, insulated from possibility of corruption, and immune to political pressure.

THE COURT'S MODE OF WORKING

The work of the magistrates and assessors was not easy. The workload was very heavy. The court processed many thousands of cases every year. There was no limitation, either in subject matter or in amount at issue, to the type or size of case that might come before it. The problems it was called upon to resolve were very varied and could be very difficult. They could raise highly complex and esoteric issues that might well have daunted much more prestigious tribunals than the Mixed Court.

The assessors for their part strove constantly to ensure that the court acted in all its roles according to the principles of the adjudicative systems of Western jurisprudence applying "Chinese law" or "the laws of China," and the court claimed consistently that it was doing so. But this claim needs qualification. On closer examination it proves to consist more of illusion than of substantive fact. The court was not the creature of any sovereign power and was not bound by the transcendent imperatives of any sovereign power. In fact there did not exist any such corpus of fixed and universal imperatives as the phrase "laws of China" implies. The proceedings of the court were not governed by any such framework of ineluctable rules as is required to provide a foundation for administration of order in the adjudicative mode. Although the court represented itself as an adjudicative tribunal, nevertheless in the final analysis its proceedings can best be interpreted, and can only be properly comprehended, in terms of disciplinary theory as a disciplinary tribunal in a group-disciplinary society in a context of contending groups.

ON THE DEBIT SIDE

A number of deficiencies and defects must be entered against the court. First among these is the lack of any court of appeal from its judgments. Numerous proposals to remedy this were suggested from time to time but none proved acceptable. The basic reason for this deficiency and for the impossibility of reform was that the court in its essential nature was a disciplinary tribunal and in disciplinary systems, as appears from our study of disciplinary theory, appeals courts are not meaningful and are unknown. Administrative reviews of decisions and punishments are regular practice in disciplinary systems, but these are always at the instance and in the interests of superior authority in the hierarchy, and their object is to make sure that leadership policies and orders are being observed.

Thus in the case of the International Settlement the consuls would sometimes act to amend a Mixed Court decision or sentence for their own purposes, but appeals, in the sense of a motion instigated by one of the parties in that party's own interest for the correction of a decision at a higher judicial level, were unknown. The best a party could get was a rehearing.

A second serious defect in the Mixed Court system was the circumstance that consular influence and authority over the court left the way open for corruption and dishonesty on the part of the consuls of the smaller and less responsible of the treaty powers. Nothing could be done about this, because consular authority had necessarily to remain supreme, according to the structure of the International Settlement, where a consul's own nationals were concerned. It was easy for a consul to naturalize any Chinese citizen who was prepared to pay handsomely for it, thus putting that Chinese citizen beyond the power of the Mixed Court and in a situation where he could be reached only through the very consul whom he had paid to protect him.

Another unfortunate aspect of the Mixed Court system was that the consular assessors were often placed in a very invidious position on the bench. They were not independent and were subject to being called to account by their superiors for the performance of their duties. They had no security of tenure and sometimes were faced with a conflict of interest. This did nothing to improve the quality of an assessor's work or his satisfaction in the performance of it. Indeed, carried to an extreme, when a consul gave a direction it meant that the impartiality of the court which the assessors were at such pains to preserve could not be sustained, and the court's disciplinary nature was exposed.

Another grave weakness in the system was the court's inability to enforce its process and its judgments outside settlement limits without the cooperation of republican government officials. This weakness ultimately proved fatal.

THE CHINESE VIEW OF MIXED COURT PERFORMANCE

From the point of view of Chinese outside the settlement looking in, the major defect in the court's operations—a defect which vitiated its whole performance in their eyes—was that it did not accept direction from Chinese sources. It responded neither to Chinese government authority embodied in the directions of the commissioner for foreign affairs, nor to Chinese traditional group authority exercised by the guild officials and the gentry. The Chinese of course raised no objection at all to the court being directed by superior authority. They expected such direction as natural and proper. What they did object to was that the court took its direction from consular and not from Chinese sources.

This state of affairs brought about two things that greatly irked the Chinese. First, it meant that rich sources of taxation, revenue, and wealth in Chinese hands on Chinese soil were closed to exploitation by Chinese government agencies and by lesser group authorities. Second, it meant that political dissidents residing in the settlement were shielded from arrest and retribution for their disobedience and insubordination and were protected from government vengeance unless a crime could be proved against them. This seriously undermined the whole Chinese concept of the hierarchical structure of society, and the traditional Chinese faith in *xiao* and obedience to superiors as the cement that held society together. In Chinese eyes the intransigence of the court in this regard constituted a threat to the very basis of all organized and civilized life.

From the point of view of Chinese inside the settlement making use of the tribunal or caught up in its proceedings, its chief defect was the necessity of engaging foreign counsel, and the great expense that this occasioned. There was not, and in the nature of things could not be, any control by the court of foreign practitioners' charges. There could not be any procedure of taxation of costs because the court had no competence to deal with foreigners—only Chinese.

In this assessment we have taken no note of the emotions and passions that centered on the Mixed Court in relation to rising Chinese nationalism and to the stirring up in China of antiforeign feeling. We have been concerned only to assess the court's objective performance as an institution for maintaining order and for dispute resolution in the context of the development of the International Settlement and of greater Shanghai in the China of 1911–27.

SUMMARY

Summarizing, it may be said that the Mixed Court was an ad hoc creation specially fabricated to do a particular job. Its job was to maintain order among Chinese, protect Chinese, and resolve disputes among Chinese in the settlement. This job it did well, although its performance was not entirely without blemish or defect. The court owed no allegiance to any specific sovereign power and rested on no constitutional foundation. The body to which it owed its immediate existence and which defined the limits of its powers and its procedures—the consular body—was itself a mere ad hoc collective without any corporate existence, any sovereign power over Chinese, or any constitutional validity.

The Mixed Court was, in the final analysis, a disciplinary tribunal exercising control over a societal group—the Chinese in the International Settlement—who, basically, understood and wanted only the concepts, sanctions, and procedures of the disciplinary mode of order maintenance.

The Mixed Court can easily be, and often is, misjudged and misinterpreted by regarding it in terms of Western jurisprudence as the instrumentality of a conventional adjudicative system. In fact in many respects it represents rather an abortive attempt to apply the adjudicative mode in a disciplinary situation. Its history affords a concrete example in practice of what we are led in theory to expect, namely the impossibility of arriving at any simple amalgam of the two types of system or any easy reconciliation between them.

The Mixed Court depended for its existence and for its direction and control upon the hierarchical and military superiority of the Western nations, particularly Great Britain, over the Chinese. When British superiority began to falter and to fail in the face of rising nationalist sentiment in China and declining military strength in Britain, the Mixed Court could no longer sustain its own competence and simply went out of existence.

CHAPTER 8

Wider Issues

It remains to assess the work of the Mixed Court in relation to two wider issues. First, What contribution, if any, did the Mixed Court make to the solution of Keeton's problem discussed in the first chapter of this book? Keeton asked the questions, "How can Chinese law be drawn into the mainstream of the world's legal progress? How can Chinese jurisprudence be linked up with that of the West?" Second, What contribution, if any, did the Mixed Court make to the modernization of Chinese thought patterns?

For over sixty years—from 1864 to 1926—the assessors on the Mixed Court strove constantly to find an answer to the questions Keeton propounded. Throughout this period they tried earnestly and conscientiously to weave Western practices and Western principles into the Chinese pattern of dispute resolution and the maintenance of order in the Mixed Court. They failed. They were quite unable to arrive at any body of principles and rules, or any general pattern of dispute resolution and the maintenance of order, that would prove acceptable both to Chinese and at the same time to Western interests and scales of values. No amalgam of the two contrasting systems occurred. Even in the very limited field of commercial disputes, nothing in the nature of a common code—a *lex mercatoria*—arose. At the end of 1926 when the Mixed Court was abolished, the magistrate and the assessors—representing the Chinese system and the Western system—were as far apart as ever.[1] Like oil and water, the systems had been able to mix, up to a point, for limited purposes, but always remained in fact discrete, and, left to themselves, tended rapidly to separate cleanly out again. The Chinese system, at the level of the Mixed Court, simply refused to be drawn into the mainstream of Western jurisprudence.

In terms of Keeton's problem, the Mixed Court experience offered no solutions. The achievements of the Mixed Court, unfortunately, did not include, as Kotenev asserted they did, the creation of a "new type of International judicial tribunal . . . absolutely unique in its form and practice."[2] The Mixed Court was in essence a very well-known and ancient type of tribunal, the group-disciplinary type. Its procedures and concepts made no substantial contribution to the development of international and intercultural dispute resolution generally. The court offers useful parallels only to the group-disciplinary situation in the ancient institution of the autonomous trading enclave, which is very rarely to be found in operation in the present day.

But if the Mixed Court failed to arrive at a solution to Keeton's problem, the study of it has enabled us to see much more clearly what the problem is and where it lies. In the perspectives of the Mixed Court experience, Keeton's problem can be reformulated on a much broader basis and at a fundamental level. Keeton saw it as a problem in comparative law. We can now see, however, that the problem was one, not of reconciling two different systems of law at the level of the rules, but of reconciling two different systems of order at the level of the philosophical concepts underlying each. These systems, we found, were the adjudicative and the disciplinary, of which only the adjudicative is a legal system comprehensible in terms of jurisprudence. Reconciling these systems is not a problem in comparative law. The formulation of an analytical framework, of a vocabulary and conceptual constructs, that will embrace them both, if it is to be made at all, must be made at a much deeper level than that of the rules of dispute resolution and criminal administration. It must be made at the level of the philosophical and cosmological concepts of the nature and purpose of order in the universe. This takes the further consideration of the problem far beyond the scope of the present study. The kinds of differences that separate the two systems in philosophic thought have been hinted at above in chapter one, but questions at this level cannot be further pursued here. At the present day, and for practical purposes, the reconcilement of the Chinese and the Western systems remains, to us, as much in the realm of wishful thinking as it was to the Mixed Court in the 1920s.

But if we cannot yet combine any better than the Mixed Court could the Western and the Chinese systems of dispute resolution within the same analytical framework, we can at least distinguish the systems, clearly, adequately, and decisively. We can do this by recognizing that the Chinese system is *not* an adjudicative or legal system at all but a disciplinary one, and therefore can only be studied and discussed properly and meaningfully in terms of the theory of disciplinary systems, not in terms of Western jurisprudence.

It is true that the "Science of the Theory and Philosophy of Disciplinary Systems of Dispute Resolution and the Maintenance of Social

Order" still awaits two things: a short, convenient, and distinctive name; and the advent of some latter-day John Austin to write an authoritative and definitive *Province of Disciplinary Theory Determined*. It should be emphasized that disciplinary theory is not a mere subdivision of jurisprudence. It exists in its own right quite outside and quite independently of jurisprudence. It rests on quite different jural postulates, and it deserves its own name to signal this disparity.

If one were to venture to coin a word of classical derivation by analogy with the word "jurisprudence," perhaps the most accurate label one could invent for disciplinary theory would be *obsequiiprudence*.[3] Just as jurisprudence explores and emphasizes the key functions of law in the adjudicative concept of social order, so obsequiiprudence explores and emphasizes the key functions of hierarchical subordination in the disciplinary concept of social order. But obsequiiprudence is a somewhat ungainly word and hardly seems likely to win popular acceptance. Doubtless the science of disciplinary theory will attract its own name to itself, if and when it attracts scholars to its study.

But the lack of a name and of an authoritative treatment of the subject need not deny us the benefits that a recognition of its existence and an acquaintance with its broad principles afford. Indeed it may be asserted that only an extremely distorted picture and a grave misunderstanding of Chinese processes of dispute resolution and the maintenance of order in society are possible without the insights of the theory of disciplinary systems.

What part did the Mixed Court play in the introduction into China of modern Western ideas and techniques of dispute resolution and the maintenance of social order?

Rhoads Murphey has made a study of the treaty ports, of which Shanghai was the premier, in their role as "beachheads of an alien system."[4] He assessed their effectiveness or ineffectiveness as entry points for the injection into Chinese thought and practice of Western ideas of commercialization and modernization in the economic sphere. He found that the foreign presence in the treaty ports had only the smallest influence upon the traditional patterns of business and commercial affairs in China. "The great majority of Chinese were unaffected directly or indirectly in their way of life. . . . Materially China went on behaving for the most part as it always had done."[5] Murphey observed that "there was no blending of China and the West—only a sharpening of confrontation."[6] The treaty ports, with their innovations and new ways of life, were resented and rejected by the great majority of Chinese as alien and threatening. Studies in the sphere of dispute resolution and the maintenance of order in society lead to the same sort of conclusions as Rhoads Murphey arrived at in the economic sphere.

For many years prior to 1927, the Chinese had been afforded no lack of opportunity to study and to participate in the proceedings of Western adjudicative systems of order and dispute resolution in actual operation on Chinese soil. For sixty-two years His Britannic Majesty's Supreme Court for China, and for twenty years the United States Court for China, with their subordinate and subsidiary courts, had been sitting daily in the International Settlement at Shanghai. They exercised over their own nationals every kind of jurisdiction.

Very often Chinese were plaintiffs, injured parties, or witnesses, or otherwise closely involved in the proceedings, which were at all times conducted according to the highest ideals of Western jurisprudence. These courts were scrupulous in their impartiality. Research has shown that Chinese plaintiffs got the same treatment from the court as English plaintiffs did, that the judges were not prejudiced against them, and that they had the same chance of succeeding as if they had been English.[7]

Beside these strictly Western courts, the Mixed Court had offered for fifteen years a standing exhibition of the application of the Western system in the adjudicative mode to Chinese nationals in large numbers. The operations of the Mixed Court afforded to Chinese in China practical experience in all categories, whether as magistrates, counsel, parties, witnesses, or otherwise, of the Western ideology in action.

True, under our close examination, the Mixed Court does not present the same unblemished image of judicial independence that the assessors liked to think it did. In fact it was, ultimately, under the consuls' thumb, but this was not obvious. In its day-to-day workings the court presented a very close facsimile of the Western notion of a judicial tribunal and certainly came close enough to it to demonstrate the stark contrast between the Chinese and the Western concepts.

How far did this intimate presentation of the Western system in action on Chinese soil have any effect on the thinking of the Chinese people? To test this we may use the principle of the impartiality and independence of the judiciary as a yardstick. The notion that independence and impartiality are of the essence in a judge's function and are inviolable lies at the heart of the theory and practice of adjudicative systems of order. The whole edifice of Western legal theory rests for its practical application upon the premise of an independent bench and bar, uninfluenced by any fear or favor even of the sovereign political power itself.[8] The degree to which this notion prevails is a fair measure of the degree to which the adjudicative system has been accepted.[9]

To test the position in China in 1928 it is instructive to consider the case of the dismissal of Lu Xingyuan.[10] Lu was appointed president of the Provisional Court of Jiangsu in May 1927. He was of the highest integrity, honesty, and ability, he was dedicated to his work as a lawyer, and he gained the respect of all classes of the community, both Chinese and foreign.[11] He had obtained his degree of Master of Arts at Oxford and had been called to the bar at Inner Temple, London.[12] But he fell foul of the Jiangsu government, and in October 1927 he was summarily dismissed from his post because he refused to take orders from the Shanghai garrison commander.[13] He refused to deliver up to the Shanghai military authorities upon command residents of the settlement suspected of being communist sympathizers. Applying in the provisional court what had been orthodox Mixed Court practice, Lu insisted that before a man sought by outside authorities could be delivered over to them in custody, there must first be established against him a prima-facie case of the commission outside the settlement of some criminal offense.

This attitude was not acceptable to the Guomindang leadership. The communist bid for control of the Nationalist movement had been violently suppressed and Jiang Jieshi's purge of the communists was under way. Some of them were sheltering from Jiang's vengeance in the International Settlement under the protection that Lu's court afforded.

To the Chinese, thinking in terms of a hierarchical, disciplinary society, it was inconceivable that a mere lowly lawyer-official should be able to defy the will of the victorious general Jiang Jieshi and thwart him of his prey. The Shanghai and Wusong garrison commander in a published statement asserted, "Lu is a Chinese official and must obey the orders of the Garrison Commander."[14] He went on to say that Lu had refused to hand over wanted men to the garrison upon demand. So Lu was dismissed.

In a speech at a dinner given in his honor upon his retirement, Lu claimed a moral victory, declared that he would continue to serve China in the best way he could, and said that his fight for judicial independence was something for the judges in Shanghai to remember.[15]

He Shizhen (Ho Shih-Chen) was appointed president of the court in place of Lu and at the ceremony when he took his seat, he and other Chinese officials made public speeches emphasizing the duty of judges to obey the orders of their political party. The new judge, He, pledged himself to abide by the decisions of the party of which he was a member—the Guomindang—and to carry out party principles. The chairman of the Shanghai branch of the Guomindang said it had been the duty of former President Lu to execute the orders of the party, that he failed to do so, and that consequently he had been dismissed.[16]

Sir Sydney Barton, reporting the details of Judge Lu's dismissal to his minister in Beijing, commented as follows:

> The story of Mr. Lu's dismissal does not make pleasant reading. . . . The independence of the judiciary is a new notion in China and though on paper it may be guaranteed, it is not backed by the weight of Chinese public opinion, whether official or otherwise, as is evident from the enclosed account of Mr. Ho's inauguration. Indeed the C.F.A. [Commissioner for Foreign Affairs] at his interview with the Consular Committee on 27th July intimated that the Chinese public saw nothing irregular in the action of the Nationalist Government, and I have seen no comment in the Chinese press which suggests any other view than that Mr. Lu was showing an unwarrantably defiant attitude toward the Nationalist authorities.[17]

A further illustration of the Chinese attitude is afforded by the case of the Sheng Estate Charitable Trust Fund.[18] Sheng Xuanhuai[19] died in Shanghai in 1916, leaving a large estate in property and investments valued at over seven million American dollars. Part of these assets, amounting to some millions of taels, was set aside by the Sheng family and vested in private trustees for public charitable purposes.

In 1926, the Nationalists, seeking money to finance Jiang Jieshi's northern expedition, began to cast covetous eyes on this fund. But the fund and the trustees were in the International Settlement and thereby protected from direct attack. They could only be got at by court order. This meant that so long as the Mixed Court survived under consular control, they were safe. But as of 1 January 1927 the Mixed Court was abolished and its place taken by the Chinese-controlled Provisional Court of Jiangsu. The way was now open for a raid on the fund. The trustees stalled the demands for money to replenish the war chest as long as they could, but the upshot of the affair was that the provisional court was ultimately directed by the Jiangsu Provincial Government to declare that the fund was public property belonging to the government, and to order the trustees of the fund to hand the assets over to government agents, or in default to suffer arrest and imprisonment until they did. The court accepted these directions and obeyed them, so that the trustees, despite vigorous protests on their own part, and on the part of the Sheng family and in the foreign press, were compelled to surrender the funds, and the trust went out of existence.

In Washington, the solicitors office of the Department of State, commenting on the Sheng case, reported to the secretary of state that it seemed clear that

> the Shanghai Provisional Court was not functioning as a court of law administering justice in accordance with law, but as a controlled agency of the Kiangsu Provincial Government in carrying out, without question, without even an appearance of judicial procedure, the wishes and instructions of the Provincial Government.[20]

Protests by foreigners were unavailing. In 1929, the American minister to China, at a meeting with the president of the judicial Yuan in the Nationalist government, protested against government interference in the decisions of Chinese courts and about a gross lack of impartiality in judges, to the great disadvantage of foreigners. The reply that he got was a reminder that the Chinese notions of justice were not the same as the American. This was coupled with a ready admission that the government did sometimes interfere with judges' decisions, but only occasionally and only in large matters, never in small everyday matters, and that Chinese judges did and would continue to discriminate severely against foreigners whenever they got the chance, until extraterritoriality was abolished.[21] What was happening, of course, was simply that the foreigners were thinking in terms of Western jurisprudence and the Chinese were still thinking in terms of disciplinary theory, in which there was no objection at all to what the Chinese were doing.

It is apparent that by 1929 at least the principle of the independence and impartiality of the judiciary had not yet become implanted in the Chinese consciousness, despite the long exposure of the Chinese people to it, and despite the efforts of the consuls and the assessors and the Mixed Court to introduce and to propagate it. It was not wanted, and it was not accepted, either at top government level or at the level of the ordinary citizen.[22] A community unwilling to recognize the principle of the independence of the bench and bar cannot be said to have accepted the adjudicative system.[23] It must be concluded that the Mixed Court did not act as an agent for the introduction or the stimulation of any significant change in traditional disciplinary attitudes and approaches to dispute resolution and the maintenance of social order in China.

By way of confirmation it may be noted that the efforts of the Chinese government itself to convert the Chinese from their traditional disciplinary way to the new Western adjudicative way of thinking met with no better success. From about 1907 the imperial court, and after 1911 the republican leaders, labored to build up in China what was designed to be a complete system of modern courts at four levels operating on adjudicative principles and administering sets of imperatives and codes of rules modeled on Western parliamentary statutes. Perhaps the strongest stimulus for the erection of this Western-style apparatus was the hope, and the promise of Western powers, that extraterritoriality would be abolished as soon as adequate systems of order enforcement and dispute resolution on Western models had been provided in China. The success of Japan in a similar situation provided a standing example and encouragement. The Chinese efforts in this project were significantly stepped up by the Nationalist government, or at least by the judicial Yuan in the Nationalist government, from about 1928 and came to look very impressive on paper.[24]

But the Western system never caught the imagination of the Chinese people and never reached down into the national consciousness. On the eve of its abolition by the communists Karl Bünger wrote, "The introduced law has met with no success to date." Private and commercial circles, he acknowledged, and the great bulk of the Chinese people, simply did not conform to the new rules, and traditional attitudes and customs continued to prevail unchanged.[25]

The Communist triumph in 1949 spelled the end of all pretense to the reception of Western jurisprudence in China. The Communist government simply abolished "all laws and judicial systems of the Guomindang"[26] and returned officially to what the Chinese people had never in reality departed from or wanted to depart from, that is, dispute resolution, criminal administration, and the enforcement of order in disciplinary tribunals subject to political direction in all things. The modern prisons that the Nationalists were developing on Western lines for the punishment of offenders changed dramatically into schools of psychological indoctrination for the reassertion of disciplinary ideals of hierarchical subordination, conformity, and obedience to superiors at all times.[27]

One is driven to the conclusion that in the long term, neither the Mixed Court nor any other court in Shanghai, not even the "modern" courts introduced by the Chinese themselves at the highest government level, had any lasting effect at all in weaning the Chinese people from the disciplinary or parental mode to the adjudicative or legal mode of order maintenance.

But in spite of the failure of the Western presence to effect any outward or visible change in the lifestyle and cultural values of the vast majority of the Chinese people, nevertheless there was, beneath the surface, a "big traffic in ideas."[28] This flow of ideas, while it brought no major shift in basic Chinese concepts in the field of dispute resolution and the maintenance of order, was psychologically of far-reaching consequences for the political and intellectual development of China.[29] The International Settlement provided political asylum and intellectual challenge for dissidents, nonconformists, and original thinkers. It provided an area offering safety and inspiration to those who opposed the prevailing orthodoxy.[30] Here was a cosmopolitan, enterprising, modernist, urban society.[31] Here was one of the few places in all China maintaining conditions where thought and philosophy could, and did, rise above the stale values of the past and take off in new and undreamed-of directions, the ends of which are not yet in sight. It was the Mixed Court that stood guardian over those conditions in the International Settlement and protected them from attack. In that sense it may be said that the Mixed Court did play an important part in keeping open channels for the communication and development of new, exotic, and exciting ideas molding China's intellectual and political history—but only, curiously enough, in fields and areas other than its own.

Notes

ABBREVIATIONS

D.F.	Decimal File: U.S. Dept. of State, Archives
F.O.	Foreign Office, Great Britain
FO	Foreign Office file, P.R.O., London
FOCP	Foreign Office Confidential Print
N.C.H.	*North China Herald, Supreme Court Reporter and Consular Gazette*
Parl.Deb.	Parliamentary Debates, Great Britain
P.R.O.	Public Record Office, London
P.P.	Parliamentary Papers, Great Britain

CHAPTER 1. ORDER WITHOUT LAW

1. Marcel Granet, *La Pensée Chinoise* (Paris: Albin Michel, 1934), 144, 589–91.

2. Jean Escarra, *Le Droit Chinois* (Beijing: Henri Vetch, 1936).

3. Joseph Needham, *Science and Civilization in China* (Cambridge: Cambridge University Press, 1956) 2: 518–83.

4. The archetype of the construct is the Jewish concept of the world as created out of chaos by the will of God, with all nature obeying the rules laid down by him for the orderly functioning of his creation. This aspect is developed in E. Zilsel, "The Genesis of the Concept of Physical Law," *The Philosophical Review* 51 (1942): 245–49. There was no creation myth and no law-giving creator god in Chinese cosmogony, or at least none survived Confucius.

5. Needham, *Science and Civilization*, 2: 287, 562, 582.

6. For the strict application of these principles in England notwithstanding a cruel and inhumane result see *Rutherford v. Richardson* [1923] A.C.1, per Lord Birkenhead at page 12. For a dramatic presentation of the strict application of these principles where an unhappy result was avoided by a legal quibble see the trial scene in *The Merchant of Venice*, act 4, sc. 1, lines 1–401.

7. H. L. A. Hart, *The Concept of Law* (Oxford: Clarendon Press, 1961), 89–96; Lon L. Fuller, *The Morality of Law*, rev. ed., (New Haven: Yale University Press, 1969), 39.

8. For this system in operation at grass-roots level in China, see Jerome A. Cohen, "Chinese Mediation on the Eve of Modernization," in *Traditional and Modern Legal Institutions in Asia and Africa*, ed. David C. Buxbaum (Leiden: E.J. Brill, 1967), 54–76. For this system in operation at top level in Japan see the discussion in chapter 2 above.

9. The word *discipline* has three main connotations. It may be used in its most precise sense to signify a means of magnifying the effectiveness of the efforts of a number of men in the achievement of a specific objective. Max Weber uses it in this way as quoted in chapter 6. It may be used to signify punishment merely, as when one speaks of a disciplinary power, meaning a power to punish for domestic misbehavior. Or it may be used in a broad sense to signify a particular mode of maintaining order in society generally. It is in this last sense that it is used in this work when we speak of a disciplinary system of order. The word has other significations that need not detain us here.

10. Alice Ehr-Soon Tay, "Law in Communist China," part 1, *Sydney Law Review* 6, no. 2 (Oct. 1969): 156.

11. Many of the autonomous religious houses of the Middle Ages were organized and managed upon the principles expressed in the *Rule* of St. Benedict written about 600 A.D. This was a disciplinary system under which total obedience was owed to the patriarchal authority of an abbot. For the text see *The Rule of St. Benedict*, trans. Richard (John) Crotty (Nedlands, W.A.: University of Western Australia Press, 1963).

12. See for a discussion H. W. R. Wade, *Administrative Law*, 5th ed. (Oxford: Clarendon Press, 1982), 501–3.

13. The image of the "father and mother official" is found in the *Shi Jing* or Book of Odes; see *Minor Odes of the Kingdom*, vol. 4, part 2, of *The Chinese Classics*, trans. James Legge (London: Oxford University Press, 1871), sect. 2, bk. 2, ode 7, stanza 3, p. 273; sect. 3, bk. 2, ode 7, stanza 1, p. 489. For the "father and mother" relationship between ruler and people in Confucian ideology see John R. Watt, *The District Magistrate in Late Imperial China* (New York: Columbia University Press, 1972), 83–91.

14. Max Weber, *Economy and Society: An Outline of Interpretive Sociology*, ed. Guenther Roth and Claus Wittich, trans. Max Rheinstein et al. (New York: Bedminster Press, 1968) 2:844–45; 3:1050.

15. Tay, "Law in Communist China," 156.

16. Jerome A. Cohen, "Due Process?" in *The China Difference*, ed. Ross Terrill (New York: Harper & Row, 1979) 254–55.

17. The words *legal* and *legality* whenever used in this work connote the idea of transcendent, rigid, universal imperatives of conduct such as form the required basis for the mode designated "legal" or "adjudicative" in the presentation in chapter 1.

18. Granet, *La Pensée Chinoise*, 590.

19. Needham, "Order Which Excludes Law," in *Science and Civilization*, 2: 290, 572–74.

20. Ibid., 287, 580, 582.

21. Ibid., 519, 544.

22. Watt, *District Magistrate*, 232.

23. For a discussion see Derk Bodde, *China's First Unifier* (Hong Kong: Hong Kong University Press, 1967), 189–206.

24. Fung Yu-lan, *A Short History of Chinese Philosophy*, ed. and trans. Derk Bodde (New York: The Macmillan Company, 1948), 157.

25. Arthur Waley, *Three Ways of Thought in Ancient China* (London: Geo. Allen & Unwin, 1939), 199.

26. Istvan Szaszy, *Conflict of Laws in the Western, Socialist and Developing Countries*, trans. J. Decsenyi (Leiden: A. W. Sijthoff, 1974), 22.

27. George W. Keeton, "Chinese Law and Historical Jurisprudence," *The Chinese Social and Political Science Review* 12 (1928):515.

28. Marc van der Valk, *An Outline of Modern Chinese Family Law* (Beijing: Henri Vetch, 1939), 10.

29. René David and John Brierley, *Major Legal Systems in the World Today*, 2d ed. (London: Stevens, 1978), 480, 488.

30. René David, chief ed., *International Encyclopedia of Comparative Law* (The Hague: Mouton, 1975), 2, chap. 1, paragraphs 7–8.

31. Yosiyuki Noda, ibid., paragraphs 193–224.

32. Antony Allott, *The Limits of Law* (London: Butterworths, 1980), 243.

33. William C. Jones, "Studying the Ch'ing Code: The Ta Ch'ing Lu Li," *The American Journal of Comparative Law* 22 (1974): 335, 356.

34. Paul Bohannan, "Ethnography and Comparison in Legal Anthropology," in *Law in Culture and Society*, ed. Laura Nader (Chicago: Aldine Press, 1972), 410–11.

35. John Henry Wigmore, *A Panorama of the World's Legal Systems* (St. Paul: West Publishing Co., 1928; Washington: Washington Law Book Co., 1936), 142–43.

36. An ethnocentric approach of this kind has long been a problem in anthropology. For a discussion see Leopold J. Pospisil, *The Ethnology of Law*, 2nd ed. (Menlo Park, Calif.: Cummings, 1978), 3–7; Laura Nader, "The Anthropological Study of Law," *American Anthropologist* 67, no. 6, part 2 (Dec. 1965): 11, 22–25. For an examination in depth of the difficult problems of methodology that arise in the comparative study of legal systems in a cross-cultural context and in relating jurisprudence to sociology, see M. B. Hooker, *Legal Pluralism* (Oxford: Clarendon Press, 1975), 6–54.

37. For William C. Jones's penetrating examination and authoritative review of this issue see his "Studying the Ch'ing Code," 330–35.

38. Escarra, *Le Droit Chinois*, 359; Needham, *Science and Civilization*, 2: 525.

39. See, for example, Field Marshal Sir William Slim, "Liberty and Discipline," *Army Journal* (Australia) 329 (Oct. 1976): 29–33; General Sir Ian Hamiliton, "Discipline," in *The Soul and Body of an Army* (London: Arnold, 1921), 91–144.

40. [1954] 1 W.L.R. 730.

41. [1964] A.C. 40.

42. Wade, *Administrative Law*, 566–67.

43. Weber, *Economy and Society*, 3: 1148–56.

44. The concept of the "folk-system" is developed in Paul Bohannan, *Justice and Judgment among the Tiv* (London: Oxford University Press, 1957).

45. F. S. C. Northrop, "Toward a Deductively Formulated and Operationally Verifiable Comparative Cultural Anthropology," in *Cross Cultural Understanding*, ed. F. S. C. Northrop and Helen H. Livingston (New York: Harper and Row, 1964), 203–22; F. S. C. Northrop, *The Meeting of East and West* (New York: Macmillan, 1949), 447–54; F. S. C. Northrop, *The Taming of the Nations* (New York: Macmillan, 1952), 112.

CHAPTER 2. AN INTRODUCTION TO THE STUDY OF THE PRINCIPLES OF DISCIPLINARY THEORY

1. For an example of the variety and complexity of some of the considerations that can arise in a discussion of the nature of law see Allott, 1–27.

2. Mark de Wolfe Howe, comp. *The Occasional Speeches of Justice Oliver Wendell Holmes* (Cambridge, Mass.: Belknap Press, 1962), 75.

3. Charles O. Hucker, *The Censorial System of Ming China* (Stanford: Stanford University Press, 1966), 285.

4. Ch'ü T'ung-tsu, *Law and Society in Traditional China* (The Hague: Mouton, 1961; Taiwan: Rainbow Bridge, 1965), 29.

5. George W. Paton, *A Textbook of Jurisprudence*, ed. George W. Paton and David P. Derham, 4th ed. (Oxford: Clarendon Press, 1972), 132–87.

6. Col. John Henry Wigmore, "Some Lessons for Civil Justice to Be Learned from Federal Military Justice," *Maryland State Bar Association Transactions* 24 (1919): 188.

7. General Dwight D. Eisenhower addressing the New York Lawyers Club 17 November 1948, quoted by Edward F. Sherman, "Justice in the Military," in James Finn, ed., *Conscience and Command* (New York: Random House, 1971), 27.

8. John Henry Wigmore, *Law and Justice in Tokugawa Japan*, pt. 1 (Tokyo: Kokusai Bunka Shinkokai, 1969), 41.

9. Asakawa Kanichi, *The Documents of Iriki* (New Haven: Yale University Press, 1929; Westport, Conn.: Greenwood Press, 1974), 132.

10. Paul H. Ch'en, *Chinese Legal Tradition under the Mongols* (Princeton: Princeton University Press, 1979), 98.

11. Jonathan Spence, *Emperor of China* (London: Jonathan Cape, 1974), 29–31.

12. George T. Staunton, trans., *Ta Tsing Leu Lee; Being the Fundamental Laws . . . of the Penal Code of China* (London: Cadell and Davies, 1810; Taipei: Ch'eng-wen Publishing Co., 1966), 269–462.

13. That is in those cases where the disciplinary tradition has not yet been overtaken and suppressed (as in the Australian army) by legal encroachments.

14. Staunton, *Ta Tsing Leu Lee*, sec. 386, 419.

15. The phrase is from M. J. Meijer, *Marriage Law and Policy in the Chinese People's Republic* (Hong Kong: Hong Kong University Press, 1971), 7.

16. Frederich C. Teiwes, *Elite Discipline in China* (Canberra: Contemporary China Centre, Australian National University Press, 1978), 11–48, offers an illuminating exposition of how Chinese leaders orchestrated the complementary effects of education and punishment in a "persuasive-coercive continuum" for the rectification of deviant behavior and the maintenance of Party discipline during the years 1949–53. Teiwes's book does not touch on the theory of discipline but presents an account of the actual practices of an avowedly disciplinary system—that of the Chinese Communist Party—in action. For an account of a Chinese prison in its modern guise of an educational institution—a reform school—see Zhou Zheng and Liu Bin, "Bid Farewell to Yesterday: A Reformatory near Qinhuangdao," *Beijing Review*, no. 3 (17 January 1983): 19–25.

17. For accounts of these procedures by men who actually experienced them, see Bao Ruo-wang (Jean Pasqualini) and Rudolf Chelminski, *Prisoner of Mao* (New York: Coward McCann and Geoghegan, 1973), and the broadcast statement of Francis James, Australian journalist, transcribed in John Merson, *Culture and Science in China* (Sydney: Australian Broadcasting Commission, 1981), 238–39.

18. Glanville Williams, *Textbook of Criminal Law* (London: Stevens, 1978), 925.

19. A. F. P. Hulsewé, *Remnants of Han Law* (Leiden: E. J. Brill, 1955), 272.

20. Ibid.

21. Staunton, *Ta Tsing Leu Lee*, 269–70.

22. Bum-Joon Lee Park, "The British Experience of Counterinsurgency in Malaya: The Emergency 1948–1960" (Ph.D. diss., The American University, Washington, D.C., 1965), 159–64.

23. For decimation in the Roman Army see G. R. Watson, *The Roman Soldier* (London: Thames and Hudson, 1981), 119–20.

24. Clifford Walton, *History of the British Standing Army, A.D. 1660 to 1700* (London: Harrison & Sons, 1894).

25. Ch'ü, *Law and Society*, 74–76.

26. For amnesties in Chinese history viewed against the background of a legal, not a disciplinary, system see Brian E. McKnight, *The Quality of Mercy:*

Amnesties and Traditional Chinese Justice (Honolulu: The University Press of Hawaii, 1981).

27. Father Bonnichon, who was a professor of law and had personal experience of the disciplinary system of order in China in 1954 looked on this principle as an atrocious Communist invention. See André Bonnichon, *Law in Communist China* (The Hague: International Commission of Jurists, circa 1956), 4, 8, 11, 27. Of course it was not. It was no more than, and no less than, one of the common principles of the theory of disciplinary systems.

28. According to Bonnichon's experience in the China of 1954, to defend yourself amounted to revolt, to an attack upon the government. Arrested persons were expected to submit and confess, not to defend themselves. Bonnichon, *Law in Communist China*, 3–6, 10.

29. Wu Ching-tzu, *The Scholars* (Beijing: Foreign Languages Press, 1957), 666–67.

30. Hart, *Concept of Law*, 95.

31. For an example where the emperor, considering a case before him, changed the rule and applied the changed rule ex post facto to the previously committed offense see Derk Bodde and Clarence Morris, *Law in Imperial China: Exemplified by 190 Ch'ing Dynasty Cases* (Cambridge, Mass.: Harvard University Press, 1967), 359–62. For a case where the emperor was persuaded to follow the code for the sake of consistency, ibid., 174–75, 502.

32. For a comprehensive, illuminating, and authoritative account of the *Kujikata Osadamegaki* see Dan F. Henderson and Yoshiro Hiramatsu, *Administration of Justice in Tokugawa Japan: Translation of* Written Provisions Concerning Suits *(Kujikata Osadamegaki) Book I (1742)*. Publication of this study has been delayed by the untimely death of Professor Hiramatsu, but the introduction has been published. See Dan Fenno Henderson, "Introduction to the Kujikata Osadamegaki (1742)," in Editorial Committee for Memorial Essays in Honor of Dr. Hiramatsu Yoshiro, *Hô to keibatsu no rekishi-teki kosatsu* (Historical studies on law and punishment) (Nagoya: Nagoya Daigaku Shuppankai, 1987), 489–544.

33. Ibid., Uses of the Osadamegaki, 508.

34. Ibid., 505.

35. F.O. "Memorandum by Sir John Pratt respecting the Chinese Courts in the International Settlement at Shanghai," FO 371/16197 f. 392, pp. 6–9.

36. The phrase is from Dan F. Henderson, "The Evolution of Tokugawa Law," in *Studies in the Institutional History of Early Modern Japan*, ed. John W. Hall and Marius B. Jansen (Princeton: Princeton University Press, 1968), 214.

37. The phrase is from Henry Sumner Maine, *Dissertation on Early Law and Custom* (London: Murray, 1883), 389.

38. In earlier European history, as Maine pointed out, "no such conception was entertained as that of 'territorial sovereignty.'" Maine, *Ancient Law* (1861; reprint, London: Oxford University Press, 1950) 85.

39. David J. Steinberg et al., *In Search of Southeast Asia: A Modern History* (New York: Praeger, 1971), 7.

40. In modern times since the ascendency of law over discipline, and under conditions of peace, this is generally arranged beforehand and given recognition and legal validity by formal diplomatic exchanges between the sovereign powers involved.

41. For analogous attitudes toward dispute resolution in the disciplinary and hierarchical context of Japanese Tokugawa society under its "rule-by-status" see Henderson and Hiramatsu, *Osadamegaki*, Introduction, "Jurisprudence," 504.

42. The phrase "didactic conciliation" is from Dan F. Henderson, *Conciliation and Japanese Law: Tokugawa and Modern* (Seattle: University of Washington Press, 1965), 1–6, 55–56, 240.

43. Ibid.; Cohen, "Chinese Mediation."

44. H. F. Handley-Derry, "Chinese Civil Cases," report of 11 May 1912 enclosed in Fraser to Jordan, 11 May 1912, FO 671/347; FO 228/2516, p. 9 of the report.

45. Ibid., Appendix 3 to the report.

46. Ibid.

47. In China it was quite possible when a new district surrogate was appointed, to bring up again an old dispute before him in the hope that he might give a different decision from his predecessor. See Watt, *District Magistrate*, 217. At page 219 Watt refers to a *tsu* quarrel which was reopened and reargued every year for ten years.

48. This principle was applied in the Mixed Court in 1924. See discussion in chapter 6 above.

49. See discussions in chapters 6 and 7 above.

50. For these rules see Hu Hsien Chin, *The Common Descent Group in China and Its Functions* (New York: Viking Fund, 1948; reprint, New York: Johnson, 1964), 62–63, 162–63; see particularly articles 15, 16, 19, 20.

51. [1977] 1 All E.R. 696.

52. Ibid., pp. 718, 719.

53. [1977] 3 All E.R. 70.

54. Brisbane *Courier-Mail*, 8 June 1983, p. 11.

55. Karl A. Wittfogel, *Oriental Despotism* (New Haven: Yale University Press, 1957), 101–60.

56. "The Report of H.M. Commissioners for Enquiring into the System of Military Punishments in the Army—Delivered Mar. 15, 1836," *P.P.* 1836, 22, question 5834, p. 351.

57. For detailed analyses and interpretations of the psychological and philosophical factors that underlie the establishment and persistence of a hierarchical disciplinary society, and for the way they were and are engendered and cultivated in Chinese society, see Richard H. Solomon, *Mao's Revolution and the Chinese Political Culture* (Berkeley: University of California Press, 1971).

58. For a study of the mutually dependent relationship between British officers and Indian troops see Jeffrey Greenhut, "Sahib and Sepoy: An Enquiry into the Relationship of the British Officers and Native Soldiers of the British Indian Army," *Military Affairs* (U.S.A.) 48, no. 1 (Jan. 1984):15–18.

59. Escarra, *Le Droit Chinois*, 7.

60. R. W. M. Dias, *Jurisprudence* (London: Butterworths, 1970).

61. Paton, *A Textbook of Jurisprudence*, 72–73.

62. Dan F. Henderson, "Japanese Influences on Communist Chinese Legal Language," in Jerome A. Cohen, ed., *Contemporary Chinese Law: Research Problems and Perspectives* (Cambridge, Mass.: Harvard University Press, 1970), 167.

63. Bonnichon, *Law in Communist China*, 12.

64. Ibid., 3.

65. C. E. Brand, *Roman Military Law* (Austin: University of Texas Press, 1968), xiii.

66. It is not impossible of course in a national emergency for a lawyer to accept discipline and become a successful soldier. Edmund Herring K. C. rose to the rank of Lieutenant-General with command of an Australian army corps on active service in wartime. He later became Sir Edmund Herring K.C.M.G., Chief Justice of the State of Victoria. See Stuart Sayers, *Ned Herring* (Melbourne: Hyland House, 1980). Many other examples could be quoted.

67. Hulsewé, *Remnants of Han Law*, preface, 1.

CHAPTER 3. THE DISTRICT MAGISTRATE

1. "Judge" Bao Zheng represents the paragon of a fair and compassionate disciplinary administrator in the folklore and literature of imperial China. For a picture of the horrible pains and suffering he was accustomed to inflict as a matter of routine upon accused and witnesses, the innocent and the guilty alike, in the course of his procedures at his most sympathetic, see the play *A Dream of Butterflies*, act 2, the trial scene, in H. C. Chang, ed. and trans., *Chinese Literature: Popular Fiction and Drama* (Edinburgh: Edinburgh University Press, 1973), 70–72. The play is from the northern drama of the Yuan period and dates from about the mid-thirteenth century.

2. Katrina C. D. McLeod and Robin D. S. Yates, "Forms of Ch'in Law: An Annotated Translation of the *Feng-chen shih*," *Harvard Journal of Asiatic Studies* 41, no. 1 (June 1981): 130, n. 54; Hulsewé, *Remnants of Han Law*, 77. For this ancient identity of "confession" with submission and the implacable insistence upon it still prevailing in the disciplinary society of Mao's China, although the means adopted to compel it are different, see Bao Ruo-wang, *Prisoner of Mao*, 34–40, 59–62.

3. See for example Alison Wayne Conner, "The Law of Evidence during the Ch'ing Dynasty" (Ph.D. diss., Cornell University, 1979). Conner wrestled with the problem of "confessions" and the use of torture to get them at length

(119–212) but without arriving at any positive or well-defined rationale to support them.

4. These were, in Qing times, comprised in the *Da Qing Lu Li.*

5. Wejen Chang, "The Grand Secretariat Archive and the Study of the Ch'ing Judicial Process," *Ch'ing-shih wen-t'i* 4, no. 5 (June 1981): 112–15.

6. For this concept see J. M. Romein, "The Common Human Pattern," *Journal of World History* (Cahiers d'Histoire Mondiale) 4, no. 2 (1957): 454–63.

CHAPTER 4. THE MIXED COURT PRIOR TO 1911

1. For the research and the sources upon which this short chapter is based, see T. B. Stephens, "The History and Jurisprudence of the Mixed Court of the International Settlement at Shanghai 1911–1927" (Ph.D. diss., University of Queensland, 1985), 59–97.

2. I.e. the Daotai of the Su-Song-Tai circuit. He was the senior Chinese government official in the Shanghai area and was responsible for relations with foreigners.

3. For a penetrating study of this conflict in its wider political and sociological dimensions and significance see Mark Elvin, "The Mixed Court of the International Settlement at Shanghai (Until 1911)," in *Papers on China* (Cambridge Mass.: East Asian Research Center, Harvard University, 1963) 17:131–59.

4. See discussion in chapter 5 above.

5. Conner, "The Law of Evidence," discusses the aspects of Qing evidentiary procedure that seemed most questionable and most dangerous in the eyes of Western lawyers, and traces the safeguards against error that existed at least in theory and on paper, even if they may not always have been applied in practice.

CHAPTER 5. THE MIXED COURT 1911–27

1. The sudden change of allegiance was of course premeditated and had been the subject of much prior maneuver and intrigue. See Mark Elvin, "The Revolution of 1911 in Shanghai," in *Papers on Far Eastern History* (Canberra: Department of Far Eastern History, Australian National University, March 1984), 29: 119–61.

2. Report by the sub-inspector of police stationed at the Mixed Court to the Municipal Council, *N.C.H.*, 8 July 1911, 108; *N.C.H.*, 18 May 1912, 456.

3. At this time there were hundreds of different kinds of taels of different values current in China. The one referred to here is the "Shanghai tael sycee." At the rate of exchange offered by the banks in Shanghai in 1911, sixty thousand such taels would have been the equivalent of approximately thirty-six thousand United States dollars of that time. This sum amounted to about six times the annual salary paid by the consuls to the magistrate whom they appointed to succeed Bao.

4. For Fraser's report of these events see Fraser to Jordan, 11 Nov. 1911,

FO 371/1310, ff. 296–302. For a copy of the actual document signed by the consuls see Appendix I, Handley-Derry's report on "Chinese Civil Cases," FO 228/2516.

5. *N.C.H.*, 18 Nov. 1911, 448.

6. For an interpretation of their course of action in terms of group-disciplinary theory see discussion in chapter 6 above.

7. Senior consul to the Mixed Court Magistrate, 1 Dec. 1911, quoted verbatim from consular body correspondence by J. E. Jacobs in *Memorandum for the American Commissioner on the Extraterritoriality Commission*, Washington: Dept. of State, Division of Publications, series D, no. 81, China no. 38, 15 July 1925. D.F. 793.003C73/333, p. 68.

8. For this development see Handley-Derry's report on "Chinese Civil Cases," FO 228/2516.

9. *N.C.H.*, 16 Dec. 1911, 753–54.

10. For the text of the rules see Anatol M. Kotenev, *Shanghai: Its Mixed Court and Council* (Shanghai: North China Daily News and Herald, 1925), 174.

11. Fraser to Jordan, 9 Feb. 1912, enclosure, FO 671/347.

12. *N.C.H.*, 18 May 1912, 456–57.

13. *N.C.H.*, 10 June 1916, 581.

14. Mary Ninde Gamewell, *The Gateway to China*, new and rev. ed. (New York: Fleming H. Revell Co., 1916), 27.

15. H. T. Montague Bell and H. G. W. Woodhead, *The China Year Book 1913* (London: G. Routledge, 1913; Nendeln Liechtenstein: Kraus Reprint Corporation, 1974), 123; H. G. W. Woodhead, ed., *The China Year Book 1929–30* (Tianjin: Tientsin Press Limited, n.d.,) 135. At the rate of exchange quoted by the European banks in Shanghai in 1911 (average over the year) 100 Haikwan taels was the equivalent of 65 American gold dollars, so that HT11,786,662 would amount to USG$7,661,330. Similarly at the 1926 rates of exchange (HT1=USG$.76), HT33,630,877 equals USG$25,559,466.

16. For the 1912, 1913 and 1915 figures see Kotenev, *Shanghai: Its Mixed Court*, 313, 318, 317. For the 1926 figures see Shanghai Municipal Council *Annual Report 1926*, 37.

17. Kotenev, *Shanghai: Its Mixed Court*, 313, 317, 318.

18. See minutes of the meetings of assessors of 26 May 1924 and 31 Dec. 1924, and letter from the registrar to the consular body, 3 Apr. 1925 FO 656/175.

19. J. Escarra, *Droits et Interêts Etrangers en Chine* (Paris: Sirey, 1928), 42.

20. Acting consul-general at Shanghai to Secretary of State, Washington, 9 Feb. 1927, enclosure 3(a). D.F. 893.05/95.

21. John C. H. Wu, *Fountain of Justice* (Taipei: Mei Ya Publications, 1971), 19.

22. For some bizarre examples of the great breadth, variety, and complexity of the issues tried in the Mixed Court see Norwood F. Allman, "What the

Shanghai Mixed Court Is and What It Does," *China Weekly Review*, 5 July 1924, 148–49. Allman writes, "The Court has no limitations on its jurisdiction of subject matter. In fact it has a broader jurisdiction than any other Court in the world."

23. Giuseppe Domenico Musso, *La Cina ed i Cinesi: Loro Leggi e Costumi* (Milano: Ulrico Hoepli, 1926), 444–45, fn. 179; Jacobs, *Memorandum for the American Commissioner*, 68.

24. Martin to Garstin, 3 July 1914, FO 656/133.

25. See, for an example, *N.C.H.*, 10 May 1924, 226.

26. Charles Drage, *Taikoo* (London: Constable, 1970), 279. *Taikoo* is the history of John Swire & Sons, Far Eastern merchants. Commander Drage has informed me that this report is from the archives of that firm.

27. "Report of the Commission on Extra-territoriality in China (China no. 3, 1926)," Cmd. 2774, *P.P. 1926*, 8:499 ff.

28. Kotenev, *Shanghai: Its Mixed Court*, 313.

29. British assessor's correspondence file FO 656/175.

30. A copy of the roll appears in the British assessor's correspondence file for 1917, FO 656/141.

31. News item, Shanghai *Evening News*, 12 July 1926, enclosure no. 1 in Cunningham to Secretary of State, 11 Aug. 1926, D.F. 893.05/74.

32. Norwood F. Allman, *Shanghai Lawyer* (New York: McGraw-Hill, 1943), 115–16. Allman himself was fluent in more than one Chinese dialect. He was one of only three American lawyers in China who could practice in Chinese without an interpreter. He also spoke Spanish.

33. John C. H. Wu, *Beyond East and West* (New York: Sheed and Ward, 1951; reprint, Taipei: Mei Ya Publications, 1969), 133.

34. F.O. "Memorandum by Sir John Pratt," 10 Aug. 1932, FO 371/16197 f. 392.

35. Jordan to Sheppard (of Jardine Matheson) 29 Feb. 1924, enclosed in Butterfield & Swire to John Swire & Sons, 26 June 1925, Swire Archives, sec. JSSII, 2/4, box 40, item 50(a).

36. F.O. weekly summary of events in China, 3 Dec. 1926, FO 405/252A, *FOCP* 13264, p. 613.

37. F.O. "Memorandum on the Question of the Recognition of the Southern Government," 12 Dec. 1926, FO 405/252A, *FOCP* 13264, p. 636.

38. U.S. Dept. of State memorandum, "Surrender of Extraterritorial Jurisdiction in China," 15 May 1929, D.F. 711.933/48.

39. China Association Archives, Circular of Correspondence for General Committee 357, p. 4, and 360, p. 5 (Sept. 1925).

40. Chamberlain to Macleay, 20 Nov. 1925, *FOCP* 12991, p. 455.

41. Schurman to Secretary of State, 28 Mar. 1924, D.F. 893.05/32.

42. Senior Consul, Shanghai, to Diplomatic Body, Beijing, 6 May 1925, FO 405/248, *FOCP* 12991, pp. 544–47.

43. Musso, *La Cina*, 144–45, n. 179.

44. Registrar Mixed Court to Consular Body, 7 Sept. 1925, FO 656/182.

45. Senior Consul to Commissioner of Foreign Affairs, 28 Oct. 1925, FO 656/182.

46. Commissioner of Foreign Affairs to Senior Consul, 11 Nov. 1925, FO 656/182.

47. See discussion in chapter 2 above.

48. For the story of the rendition see Macleay to Chamberlain, 26 July 1926, FO 405/252A, *FOCP* 13264, pp. 208–11; U.S. Consul-General Shanghai, to Secretary of State, 5 Oct., 6 Nov., 15 Dec., and 20 Dec. 1926, D.F. 893.05/76, 79, 85, 87, and 88. Kotenev's wordy and somewhat garbled account of the rendition as it appeared to him at the time is given in his second book, *Shanghai: Its Municipality and the Chinese* (Shanghai: North China Daily News and Herald, 1927), 171–88. His account is, however, useful in that it provides in convenient form the text of the agreement for rendition and the supplementary arrangements and correspondence between the parties covering details not mentioned in the agreement.

49. F.O. memorandum on "The Question of the Recognition of the Southern Government," FO 405/252A, *FOCP* 13264, p. 637.

50. For a copy of the agreement see Acting U.S. Consul-General to Secretary of State, 20 Dec. 1926, D.F. 893.05/88. It was published in Shanghai *Municipal Gazette* 18 Feb. 1927, and reprinted in *American Journal of International Law*, 1927 Supplement, 113.

51. For the specification of these exceptions, see the terms of the supplementary arrangements come to between the parties, printed in Kotenev, *Shanghai: Its Municipality*, 184–86.

CHAPTER 6. MIXED COURT ADMINISTRATION OF ORDER ANALYZED

1. U.S. Dept. of State Archives, D.F. 893.053/2.

2. *China Law Review* 1, no. 4, (Jan. 1923): 190.

3. *In the Matter of the Trusts of Certain Property: Duncan McNeill and Loftus Edward Percival Jones Trustees, North China Daily News* 22 June 1914, p. 10; 1 July 1914, p. 12.

4. Kotenev, *Shanghai: Its Mixed Court*, ix, xi, 276.

5. Escarra, *Droits et Interêts*, 43; "The Extra-territoriality Problem," *China Law Review* 2, no. 1 (July 1924): 18–19.

6. "Report of the Commission on Extra-territoriality in China," para. 23.

7. Westel W. Willoughby, *Foreign Rights and Interests in China*, 2d rev. ed. (Baltimore: John Hopkins Press, 1927), 535.

8. *The Schooner "Exchange" v. M'Faddon and others* (1812), 7 Cranch 116 at 136; 3 U.S. Supreme Court Reports (Lawyers Edition) 287 at 293.

9. *Papayanni v. Russian Steam Navigation Co: The Laconia* II, Moore N.S.

161 at 181; 15 Eng. Rep. 862 at 870. For an authoritative treatment of the subject in the Far Eastern context at the relevant time see Sir Francis Piggott, *Extra-territoriality: the Law Relating to Consular Jurisdiction and to Residence in Oriental Countries*, new rev. ed. (Hong Kong: Kelly & Walsh, 1907), 41–43.

10. Chamberlain, H. of C., 8 July 1925, 5 *Parl. Deb*. CLXXXVI (1925) 392.

11. *Papers Relating to the Foreign Relations of the United States 1913* (Washington: U.S. Government Printing Office, 1920), 85.

12. Williams to Secretary of State, 13 Oct. 1913, ibid., 136.

13. "Case Brought on Appeal from Kiangsi 16th Day 3rd Month, 6th Year of the Chinese Republic, No. 592, Vol. 2, p. 13," translated by N. F. Allman in "Memorandum on the Mixed Court" 1 Nov. 1922, U.S. Dept. of State Archives D.F. 893.053/Sh/15.

14. *Ibid.*

15. Telegram, Schurman to Secretary of State, 11 Mar. 1924, D.F. 893.053/Sh/23.

16. Telegram, Perkins to Secretary of State, 15 Dec. 1929, D.F. 893.05/208.

17. Editorial, *China Law Review*, 1, no. 4 (Jan. 1923): 153.

18. *Buron v. Denman*, (1848) 2 Exch. 167. A useful treatment of act of state (as it was in 1934) is E. C. S. Wade, "Act of State in English Law: Its Relation with International Law," *The British Year Book of International Law* 15 (1934): 98–112. See also D. L. Kier and F. H. Lawson, *Cases in Constitutional Law*, 5th ed. (Oxford: Clarendon Press, 1967), 155–63.

19. *Johnstone v. Pedlar*, 1921 2 A.C. 262 at 290.

20. [1906] 1 K.B. 613 at 639–40.

21. *Johnstone v. Pedlar*, p. 278.

22. For the United States see *U.S. v. The Paquete Habana,* 189 US 453 at 465, 1902, approving *Buron v. Denman; Dona Maria Francisca O'Reilly de Camara, Countess of Buena Vista v. Brooke,* 209 US 45 (1907).

23. See discussion in chapter 2 above.

24. Unless, of course, for political purposes, in order to cause embarrassment to the foreigners and to promote sentiments of nationalism.

25. See discussion in chapter 2 above.

26. *In re Ming Sung Umbrella Factory Winding-Up—Barlow and others v. Yen Siao Hong and others* (1926) *N.C.H.* 20 Mar. 1926, 538.

27. Acting Registrar to P. Grant Jones, 29 May 1919, *et seq.*, FO 656/146.

28. *Zee Van-kao v. Kao Yao-ding* (1925) *N.C.H.* 28 Feb. 1925, 362.

29. Annex III to F.O. "Memorandum on the International Municipal Government of Shanghai," 27 July 1925 FO 405/248, *FOCP* 12991, p. 83.

30. Jacobs, *Memorandum for the American Commissioner*, 76.

31. *N.C.H.* 26 Oct. 1912, 233.

32. *N.C.H.* 25 Apr. 1925, 158.

33. J. E. Jacobs, "The Legality of China's So-Called New Laws," 23 Dec.

1925, in "File of Documents and Papers used by Silas H. Strawn U.S. Commissioner on the International Commission on Extraterritoriality in China 1925–26." Enclosure 1, vol. 7, Laws of China D.F. 793.003C73/333.

34. Wang Chonghui, "Observations of the Chinese Commissioner on the Relation between the Constitution and the Laws of China," 12 July 1926, ibid.

35. "Report of the Commission on Extra-territoriality in China," paras. 58, 109, 110, 199–202.

36. Ibid., note to heading part II, sec. III, para. 59.

37. For a copy of this report see FO 371/7983, f. 240.

38. "Report of the Commission on Extra-territoriality in China," para. 115.

39. Ibid., paras. 74–76.

40. Ibid., paras. 203–4.

41. Georges Padoux, "List of English and French Translations of Modern Chinese Laws and Regulations," *Chinese Social and Political Science Review* 19 (1936): 567–604.

42. See discussion in chapter 2 above.

43. *N.C.H.* 25 Apr. 1925, 158.

44. Blackburn to Shields (Postal Commissioner), 10 Jan. 1922 FO 656/170.

45. These are printed in Kotenev, *Shanghai: Its Mixed Court*, 557–75. They originated in 1845 in rules made and promulgated by the Daotai and the British Consul at Shanghai for the establishment of a small precinct or settlement area where the foreigners would be permitted to live and trade, and for the orderly government and management of the internal affairs of the settlement by the foreigners themselves. The area was later extended and the regulations amended.

46. These amounted to edicts or standing orders issued from time to time by the municipal council on a great variety of subjects for the better government of municipal affairs. They were enforced by the council against Chinese in the Mixed Court. There was no specific authority for the issue and enforcement of these edicts and orders, neither in the land regulations nor elsewhere, except in the limited areas of traffic control and building.

47. *W. Keswick and others v. Wills and Wills* (1865) *N.C.H.* 18 Nov. 1865, 182–83.

48. *Municipal Police v. Fuller* (1925) *N.C.H.* 25 Apr. 1925, 158.

49. Proclamation of Daotai Lan, 24 Feb. 1855, reprinted in Richard Feetham, *Report of the Hon. Richard Feetham C. M. G. Judge of the Supreme Court of the Union of South Africa to the Shanghai Municipal Council* (Shanghai: North China Daily News and Herald, 1931) 1:50.

50. Ibid., 67.

51. For the text in English translation of the Provisional Criminal Code as it was promulgated in 1912 see T. T. Yuen and Tachuen S. K. Loh, trans., *The Provisional Criminal Code of the Republic of China* (Beijing: Peking Gazette, 1915). This version was subsequently revised, amended, and reissued by the

Ministry of Justice in 1919. For the revised code and the mandate see *The Provisional Criminal Code of the Republic of China* (Peking: The Commission on Extraterritoriality, 1923). This text and the mandate are republished in Kotenev, *Shanghai: Its Mixed Court*, 386–425.

52. See for example *Opium Testing Office v. Van Kyi-nyo* (1916) in Kotenev, *Shanghai: Its Municipality*, 279–80 (fine of five thousand taels); *Opium Testing Office v. Tung Ah-nyi* (1916) ibid. (fine of ten thousand taels and three months imprisonment).

53. The decisions were published in December 1919 by the Supreme Court Editorial Office in three volumes, which are not available in translation. A selection was made, translated into English by F. T. Cheng, and published by the Commission on Extraterritoriality in 1923, and was reprinted in Kotenev, *Shanghai: Its Mixed Court*, 431 ff. For the interpretations, and for the distinction between the interpretations and the decisions, see M. H. van der Valk, trans. and ed., *Interpretations of the Supreme Court at Peking—Years 1915 and 1916* (Batavia: Sinological Institute, University of Indonesia 1949), 6–14.

54. In the Ming Sung Umbrella case, the magistrate and the assessor differed sharply on this point, but neither advanced any very convincing or conclusive authority or argument to support his stand; see T. B. Stephens, "The Ming Sung Umbrella Case," *Australian Journal of Politics and History* 33, no. 2 (1987): 76–89. For a short treatment of the place of precedent in the system of modern courts in China in 1925 see C. H. Chang, Y. C. Liang, and John C. H. Wu, "Sources of Chinese Civil Law," *China Law Review* 2, no. 5 (July 1925): 209–13. The "Report of the Commission on Extra-territoriality in China," paras. 77 and 117 (14), recommended that the authority of the decisions of the Supreme Court should be put beyond doubt.

55. *The Chinese Supreme Court Decisions*, no. 1, 2d year A.C. 64, in Kotenev, *Shanghai: Its Mixed Court*, 431. This formula came from the first draft for a civil code of the Republic of China of 1911 and derives from a Japanese statute of 1875; M. H. van der Valk, "Custom in Modern Chinese Private Law," *Monumenta Serica* 30 (1972–73): 222; Hozumi Nobushige, *Lectures on the New Japanese Civil Code as Material for the Study of Comparative Jurisprudence*, 2d ed. rev. (Tokyo: Maruzen Kabushiki-Kaisha, 1912), 38; Henderson, "Japanese Influences," 159–60, 177–78. The formula, or something like it, has long been a familiar one in civil law systems. For a list of some forty instances of civil codes directing the application of "general principles" or "natural law" in the absence of a specific law see Bin Cheng, *General Principles of Law* (London: Stevens, 1953), 400–408.

56. Chang, Liang, and Wu, "Sources of Chinese Civil Law," translate *tiao li* as "principles of reason and right" and say that in the search for these principles the judge is usually guided by "approved legal doctrine" and "he is to avail himself of the precedents and Draft Civil Code" (211).

57. For examples see *Burroughs Welcome and Co. v. Nanyang Medical Coy.*

(1919), *British Chamber of Commerce Journal* (Shanghai) 4.4, May 1919, pp. 29–31; *Caldbeck Macgregor & Co v. Li Yung-k'uei* (1915), *N.C.H.* 18 Sept. 1915, 787.

58. See "Report of the Commission on Extra-territoriality in China," para. 76.

59. Kotenev, *Shanghai: Its Mixed Court*, 261.

60. Garstin to Fraser 26 Feb. 1914, FO 656/133.

61. *Mun. Police v. Two Undesirables* (1927) *N.C.H.* 15 Jan. 1927, 75.

62. *N.C.H.*, 29 Sept., 6 Oct., 13 Oct. 1917.

63. See discussion in chapter 2 above.

64. FO 656/175, 24 July 1924.

65. Commissioner for Foreign Affairs to Senior Consul, 29 July 1924, FO 656/175.

66. In Tianjin a Chinese sued two German doctors for damages for the death of his wife, whom the doctors had been treating. They sought to call witnesses to show that they had not been negligent. The Chinese judge said: "I do not need witnesses. You are rich and he is poor and he has lost his wife. You should pay him something." It was with difficulty that the judge was persuaded to hear the witnesses and to absolve the doctors from any blame for the death of the woman. Article in *Japan Chronicle*, July 1925, reprinted in *Peking Leader*, 21 Aug. 1925, enclosure in Palairet to Chamberlain, 1 Oct. 1925, FO 405/248, *FOCP* 12991, p. 422.

67. *The Osceola*, 189 U.S. 158 at 175.

68. 336 U.S. 511 at 517.

69. *N.C.H.* 21 Aug. 1915, 482–84. Quoted passage is on page 483.

70. *Rizaeff Frères v. Sovtorgflot* (1926) *N.C.H.* 20 Feb. 1926, 347. *Rizaeff Frères v. Sovtorgflot—rehearing*, *China Law Review* 3, no. 6 (Oct. 1927): 14–19.

71. *N.C.H.* 1 May 1920, 287; 5 June 1920, 615.

72. Kotenev, *Shanghai: Its Mixed Court*, 224.

73. Ibid., 230.

74. Ibid., 231–32.

75. *Ex parte the Gold and Silversmiths Guild: Application to vary order* (1915) *N.C.H.* 20 Nov. 1915, 548–49 at p. 549.

76. *Dan Jau-ding v. Dsung Yuing-hsien* (1924) in Kotenev, *Shanghai: Its Mixed Court*, 293. This dictum was published in *N.C.H.* 1 Mar. 1924, 329.

77. Commissioner for Foreign Affairs to Mixed Court Magistrate, Oct. 1917, FO 656/141.

78. *N.C.H.* 4 Jan. 1919, 27–28.

79. *N.C.H.* 12 Jan. 1924, 60–61.

80. *N.C.H.* 9 June 1917, 570.

81. *Mun. Police v. Liu Fubiao* (1912) *N.C.H.*, 27 Apr. 1912, 223–25.

82. *N.C.H.* 27 Mar. 1926, 588; 1 May 1926, 200.

83. *McNeill Jones and another v. Shu Te King Ssu* (1913) *N.C.H.* 22 Nov. 1913, 572–76.

84. *In the Matter of the Trusts of certain property: Duncan McNeill and Loftus Edward Jones trustees* (1914), *North China Daily News*, 22 June 1914, 10; 1 July 1914, 12.

85. *N.C.H.* 11 July 1914, 77.

86. *N.C.H.* 14 Dec. 1912, 725. *Municipal Gazette* 14 Nov. 1912.

87. *Municipal Police v. Two revolutionaries* (1911) *N.C.H.* 18 Nov. 1911, 451, 455.

88. Memo, Barton to Martin, 18 Dec. 1925, FO 656/182.

CHAPTER 7. ASSESSMENT OF THE WORK OF THE MIXED COURT, 1911–27

1. Mark Elvin, "The Mixed Court of the International Settlement at Shanghai (Until 1911)," in *Papers on China* (Cambridge, Mass.: East Asian Research Center, Harvard University, 1963), 17: 131–59.

2. *China Weekly Review*, 5 July 1924, 148–49.

3. Randall T. Bell, "The Shanghai Mixed Court and the Staple Court of England: An Historical Comparison," unpublished paper submitted to Professor Jerome A. Cohen, Harvard Law School, 1971. I am greatly indebted to Professor Cohen for allowing me access to this paper, and for permission to refer to it.

4. Kotenev, *Shanghai: Its Mixed Court*. See, for example, x, xii.

5. Ibid., xii.

6. Ibid., 220–34. For the Ming Sung Umbrella case see notes 26 and 54 in chapter 6.

7. Manley O. Hudson, "The Rendition of the International Mixed Court at Shanghai," *The American Journal of International Law* 21 (1927): 451–71.

8. Ibid., 456.

9. Ibid., 451.

10. Ibid., 454.

11. William Crane Johnstone, Jr., *The Shanghai Problem* (Stanford: Stanford University Press, 1937), 128–54.

12. H. G. W. Woodhead, ed., *China Year Book 1926–27* (Tianjin: Tientsin Press Limited, n.d.), 1012.

13. Mark Elvin, "The Administration of Shanghai," in *The Chinese City between Two Worlds*, ed. Mark Elvin and G. William Skinner (Stanford: Stanford University Press, 1974), 246, 247, 260.

14. Feetham, *Report*, 1:103–7.

15. Sir Eric Teichman, *Affairs of China: A Survey of the Recent History and Present Circumstances of the Republic of China* (London: Methuen, 1938), 156. By "Shanghai" Teichman means the International Settlement at Shanghai.

CHAPTER 8. WIDER ISSUES

1. See T. B. Stephens, "The Ming Sung Umbrella Case," *Australian Journal of Politics and History* 33, no. 2 (1987): 76–89.

2. Kotenev, *Shanghai: Its Mixed Court*, x–xi, 275, 282.

3. I am indebted to Professor J. Duncan M. Derrett for the invention of this word.

4. Rhoads Murphey, *The Outsiders: The Western Experience in India and China* (Ann Arbor: University of Michigan Press, 1977), 227.

5. Ibid., 226–27.

6. Ibid., 225.

7. Roger Du Brock, "A Study of the Treatment Accorded to Chinese Plaintiffs in the Civil Summary Division of H.B.M.'s Supreme Court for China and Japan from 1875 to 1885 as Evidenced in the Law Reports Contained in the North China Herald," unpublished paper presented to Professor Jerome A. Cohen, Harvard University, 1967. I am grateful to Professor Cohen for showing me this paper and for permission to refer to it.

8. Jerome Cohen sketches the rise of the idea of an independent judiciary to a position of key importance in the European adjudicative system of order in "The Chinese Communist Party and Judicial Independence," *Harvard Law Review* 82, no. 5 (March 1969): 967–1007.

9. Cohen notes that the idea never achieved any significant importance in traditional or even in Nationalist Chinese thinking, ibid. 970–71, 975–76.

10. For the story of Lu Xingyuan I have relied chiefly on documents in United States Dept. of State Archives Decimal File (D.F.) 893.05 and on Sir Sydney Barton's report of the matter contained in his despatch number 158 to his minister in Beijing dated 7 August 1928, 5220/28/424, of which the draft may be found in the British assessor's correspondence file FO 656/189.

11. D.F. 893.05/113 and 131.

12. *China Year Book 1929–30*, 968.

13. D.F. 893.05/107 and 131.

14. D.F. 893.05/117.

15. D.F. 893.05/134.

16. D.F. 893.05/129.

17. Barton to Beijing, 7 August 1928, para. 12.

18. I have relied for my account of the Sheng Estate Charitable Trust fund upon the documents, reports, press cuttings, and material in D.F. 893.05/142, 158, 172 and 198, and upon the report of the affair made by the British consul-general in Shanghai to his minister in Beijing contained in despatch no. 136 of 7 May 1929, 3366/29/554, FO 656/201. This latter report includes thirty-five enclosures.

19. Sheng was generally known in his later years as Sheng Kung Pao because of his imperial honors. He was a wealthy and powerful industrial magnate with extensive railway, shipping, coal, iron, and textile interests. For his biography

see Howard L. Boorman and Richard C. Howard, *Biographical Dictionary of Republican China* (New York: Columbia University Press, 1970) 3:117–20.

20. Memorandum of 8 June 1929 by Dept. of State Solicitors Office for Secretary of State on interference with the provisional court at Shanghai by military and civil authorities, D.F. 893.05/158, p. 29.

21. Telegram, MacMurray to Secretary of State, 10 June 1929, D.F. 893.05/151.

22. Neither was it wanted nor accepted when the communists came to power in China, at least not during the first decade of communist rule; Cohen, "The Chinese Communist Party and Judicial Independence," 1005.

23. Jerome Cohen questions whether it is useful to apply contemporary Western standards of judicial independence to China, or whether some other framework of analysis might be more appropriate; ibid., 972. We have suggested in this work that at least in the context of traditional China and early Nationalist China the theory of disciplinary systems of order affords an alternative and better framework of analysis than Western legal theory.

24. See for example Escarra, *Le Droit Chinois*, viii; Franz Michael, "The Role of Law in Traditional, Nationalist and Communist China," *The China Quarterly* 9 (1962):133–34; Karl Bünger, "Die Rezeption des europaischen Rechts in China," *Deutsche Landes-referate zum III. Internationalen Kongres für Rechtsvergleichung in London 1950*, 177–81.

25. Bünger, "Die Rezeption," 181.

26. *The Common Programme* promulgated by the Chinese People's Political Consultative Conference in 1949, art. 17. Hsia Tao-tai, *Guide to Selected Legal Sources of Mainland China* (Washington: Library of Congress, 1967), 1–2.

27. For the reform prisons of communist China, see Jerome A. Cohen, *The Criminal Process in the People's Republic of China, 1949–1963* (Cambridge, Mass.: Harvard University Press, 1968), 587–618; Wei Min, "Reforming Criminals," *Beijing Review*, no. 8 (23 February 1981):22–29.

28. Rhoads Murphey, "The Treaty Ports and China's Modernization," in *The Chinese City between Two Worlds*, ed. Elvin and Skinner, 66.

29. Ibid., 18.

30. Elvin, "The Mixed Court," 147–48.

31. Marie-Claire Bergère, "The Other China: Shanghai from 1919 to 1949," in *Shanghai: Revolution and Development in an Asian Metropolis*, ed. Christopher Howe (Cambridge: Cambridge University Press, 1981), 13, 34

Select Bibliography

UNPUBLISHED PRIMARY SOURCES

Government Papers

Great Britain

Foreign Office Files at the Public Record Office, London.
FO 228/2516, Beijing Legation, correspondence.
FO 371/1310, 1927, 16197, 16199, General political correspondence.
FO 656/133, 141, 146, 170, 175, 182, 189, 201, British Mixed Court assessors' correspondence.
FO 671/334, 347, Shanghai Consulate, correspondence.

United States

Department of State Archives, Washington, Decimal Files
D.F. 711.933/48, Political relations between the U.S. and China, extraterritoriality.
D.F. 793.003, Extraterritoriality in China, negotiations.
D.F. 793.003C73/333, File of documents and papers used by Silas H. Strawn, U.S. Commissioner on the International Commission on Extraterritoriality in China, 1925–26.
D.F. 893.05/12, 34, 74, 88, 95, 107, 111, 113, 117, 124, 129, 131, 134, 141, 142, 151, 158, 172, 198, 208, Mixed Courts in China.
D.F. 893.053/2, Mixed Courts in China, jurisdiction.
D.F. 893.053/Sh./3, 5, 8, 15, 25, Mixed Courts in China, jurisdiction, Shanghai.
D.F. 893.054K, Mixed Courts in China, laws and procedure, Xiamen (Amoy)

Private Papers

China Association Archives, London.
John Swire & Sons Archives, London.

PUBLISHED PRIMARY SOURCES

Government-Originated Material

China

MacMurray, John van Antwerp. *Treaties and Agreements with and Concerning China, 1894–1919*. 2 vols. New York: Oxford University Press, 1921.

Mayers, W. F. *Treaties between the Empire of China and Foreign Powers*. 2d ed. Shanghai: North China Herald, 1897.

"Questions for Readjustment." Submission by China to the Peace Conference at Versailles 1919. Reprinted in H. T. Montague Bell and H. G. W. Woodhead, eds. *The China Year Book 1921–22*. Tianjin: Tientsin Press Limited, n.d. 2:719ff.

Great Britain

Foreign Office Confidential Prints:

FOCP 9944*

FOCP 10032, FO 405/205 (China)

FOCP 10741, FO 405/211 (China)

FOCP 10742, FO 405/212 (China)

FOCP 10759, FO 405/214 (China)

FOCP 10760, FO 405/215 (China)

FOCP 10894, FO 405/220 (China)

FOCP 12991, FO 405/248 (China)

FOCP 13103, FO 405/250 (China)

FOCP 13264, FO 405/252A (China)

Parliamentary Papers:

"The Report of H.M. Commissioners for Enquiring into the System of Military Punishments in the Army—delivered Mar. 15, 1836." *P.P.* 1836, 22:351.

"Report of the Commissioners Appointed to Enquire into the Recruiting for the Army." (1866), [3752] p. 238, *P.P.* 1867, 15:280.

Report of Assessor A. Davenport in "China No. 2, 1872, Commercial Reports from Her Majesty's Consuls in China 1870." [C. 567], pp. 57–63, *P.P.* 1872, 59:59–65.

Letter Chaloner Alabaster to Geo. F. Seward, Mar. 1875 in "China No. 5 (1875) Part II Commercial Reports by Her Majesty's Consuls in China 1874." [C. 1243–1], pp. 166–71, *P.P.* 1875, 77:728–33.

Report of C. T. Gardner in "China No. 1, Commercial Reports by Her Majesty's Consuls in China 1877–78." [C. 2231], pp. 63–78. *P.P.* 1878–79, 72:325–40.

Report of Clement F. R. Allen of 27 Aug. 1880, Wade to Granville 6 Sept. 1880, Enclosure No. 1. [C. 2881], pp. 1–5, *P.P.* 1881, 98:459–63.

"China No. 1 (1912). Correspondence Respecting the Affairs of China." [Cd. 6148], p. 77, *P.P.* 1912–13, 121:277.

"Report of the Commission on Extra-territoriality in China (China No. 3, 1926)." Cmd. 2774, *P.P.* 1926, 8:499ff.

Treaties and Conventions:

Hertslet, Lewis. *Treaties and Conventions. . . .* ("Hertslet's Commercial Treaties"). 31 vols. London: Butterworth, H.M. Stationery Office, and others, 1840–1925.

United States

Department of State:

Jacobs, J. E. *Memorandum for the American Commissioner on the Extraterritoriality Commission.* Washington: Department of State, Division of Publications, series D, no. 81, China no. 38, printed and distributed 15 July 1925. See D.F. 793.003C73/333.

Papers Relating to the Foreign Relations of the United States 1913, vol. 1, Washington: U.S. Government Printing Office, 1920.

Papers Relating to the Foreign Relations of the United States 1925, vol. 1, Washington: U.S. Government Printing Office, 1940.

U.S. Congress, *House Executive Documents*, 46th cong. 2d sess. Vol. 1, Foreign Relations, 1880, Bailey to Seward, 15 Sept. 1879, 229–31.

U.S. Congress, *House Executive Documents*, 46th cong. 3d sess. Vol. 1, Foreign Relations, 1881, George F. Seward, "Memorandum on the Mixed Court at Shanghai," 1879, 157–61.

Newspapers, Journals, and Periodicals

Annual Report (Shanghai Municipal Council), 1926.

Beijing Review (Beijing), 1981, 1983.

British Chamber of Commerce Journal (Shanghai), 1919.

China Law Review (Shanghai), 1923–27.

China Weekly Review (Shanghai), 1924.

China Year Book (London), 1913; (Tianjin), 1921–22, 1926–27, 1929–30.

Chinese Social and Political Science Review (Beijing), 1919, 1936.

Evening News (Shanghai), 1926.

Far Eastern Review (Manila), 1927.

Journal of the China Branch of the Royal Asiatic Society (Shanghai), 1887, 1889–90.

Municipal Gazette (Shanghai Municipal Council), 1927.

North China Daily News (Shanghai), 1914.

North China Herald, Supreme Court Reporter and Consular Gazette (Shanghai), 1911–26.

Books and Literary Works

Classical, Ancient, and Medieval Authors

Saint Benedict. *The Rule of St. Benedict.* Trans. Richard (John) Crotty. Nedlands, W.A.: University of Western Australia Press, 1963.

The Chinese Classics. Trans. James Legge. 5 vols. London: Oxford University Press, 1861–72. Reprint. Hong Kong: Hong Kong University Press, 1960.

Confucius. *The Analects of Confucius.* Trans. Arthur Waley. New York: Vintage Books, Random House, n.d.

Han Fei Tzu. Trans. Burton Watson. Taipei: Wen Zhi Publishing Co., 1979.

Mencius. Trans. D. C. Lau. Harmondsworth: Penguin Classics, 1970.

Sacred Books of the East. Ed. Max Muller. 49 vols. Oxford: Clarendon Press, 1881–1910.

Sun Tzu: The Art of War. Trans. Samuel B. Griffith. Oxford: Clarendon Press, 1963.

Books and Writings by Participants and Observers at First Hand

Allman, Norwood F. *Shanghai Lawyer.* New York: McGraw-Hill, 1943.

———. "What the Shanghai Mixed Court Is and What It Does." *China Weekly Review*, 5 July 1924, 148–49.

Arnold, Julean, ed. *China: A Commercial and Industrial Handbook.* Washington: Govt. Printing Office, 1926. Reprint. Taipei: Ch'eng Wen Publishing Co., 1973.

Barton, Sir Sydney. "The Shanghai Mixed Court." *Chinese Social and Political Science Review* 5 (March 1919):31–41.

Blume, W. W. "Legal Education in China." *China Law Review* 1, no. 7 (Oct. 1923):308–9.

Bryan, Robert T., Jr. *An Outline of Chinese Civil Law.* Shanghai: Commercial Press, 1925.

Chang, C. H., Y. C. Liang, and John C. H. Wu. "Sources of Chinese Civil Law." *China Law Review* 2, no. 5 (July 1925):209–13.

Darwent, The Rev. C. E. *Shanghai: A Handbook for Travellers and Residents.* 2d ed. Shanghai: Kelly & Walsh, 1920.

Editorial. *China Law Review* 1, no. 4 (Jan. 1923):153.

Escarra, Jean. *Le Droit Chinois.* Beijing: Henri Vetch, 1936.

———. *Droits et Interêts Etrangers en Chine.* Paris: Sirey, 1928.

———. "The Extra-territoriality Problem." *China Law Review* 2, no. 1 (July 1924):5–19.

Feetham, Richard. *Report of the Hon. Richard Feetham C.M.G. Judge of the Supreme Court of the Union of South Africa to the Shanghai Municipal Council.* 3 vols. Shanghai: North China Daily News and Herald, 1931.

Gamewell, Mary Ninde. *The Gateway to China.* New and revised ed. New York: Fleming H. Revell Co., 1916.

Granet, Marcel. *La Pensée Chinoise.* Paris: Albin Michel, 1934. Reprint 1950.

Ho, Chieh-Shiang. "The Mixed Court Issue: A Chinese Point of View." *China Weekly Review*, 19 July 1924, 217–18.

Hozumi Nobushige. *Lectures on the New Japanese Civil Code as Material for the Study of Comparative Jurisprudence*. 2d ed. rev. Tokyo: Maruzen Kabushiki-Kaisha, 1912.

Hsia, Ching Lin. *Studies in Chinese Diplomatic History*. Shanghai: Commercial Press, 1925.

Hung, William Shih-Hao. *Outlines of Modern Chinese Law*. N.p., 1934.

Jamieson, George. *Chinese Family and Commercial Law*. Shanghai: Kelly & Walsh, 1921.

———. "Chinese Partnerships: Liability of Individual Members." *Journal of the China Branch of the Royal Asiatic Society*, n.s. 22 (1887):39–50.

Koo, Vi Kyuin (Wellington). *The Status of Aliens in China*. New York: Columbia University Press, 1912. Reprint. New York: A.M.S. Press, 1968.

Kotenev, Anatol M. *Shanghai: Its Mixed Court and Council*. Shanghai: North China Daily News and Herald, 1925.

———. *Shanghai: Its Municipality and the Chinese*. Shanghai: North China Daily News and Herald, 1927.

Lanning, G., and S. Couling. *The History of Shanghai*. Shanghai: Kelly & Walsh, 1921.

Latter, A. M. "The Government of the Foreigners in China." *The Law Quarterly Review* 19 (1903):319–21.

"Law Fees." *British Chamber of Commerce Journal* (Shanghai) 4, no. 4 (May 1919): n.s. 1, 14.

Mayers, W. F., N. B. Dennys, and C. King. *The Treaty Ports of China and Japan*. London: Trubner, 1867.

Milne, Rev. William C. *Life in China*. London: Routledge, 1857.

Montalto de Jesus, C. A. *Historic Shanghai*. Shanghai: Shanghai Mercury, 1909.

Morse, Hosea Ballou. "Abstract of Information on Currency and Measures in China." *Journal of the China Branch of the Royal Asiatic Society* n.s. 24 (1889–90):46–135.

———. *The Trade and Administration of China*. 3d rev. ed. New York: Russell & Russell, 1920.

Musso, Giuseppe Domenico. *La Cina ed i Cinesi: Loro Leggi e Costumi*. Milano: Ulrico Hoepli, 1926.

Padoux, Georges. "List of English and French Translations of Modern Chinese Laws and Regulations." *Chinese Social and Political Science Review* 19 (1936):567–604.

Pott, F. L. Hawkes. *A Short History of Shanghai*. Shanghai: Kelly & Walsh, 1928.

Riasanovsky, V. A. *The Modern Civil Law of China*. Harbin: Zaria, 1927.

Staunton, George T., trans. *Ta Tsing Leu Lee; Being the Fundamental Laws . . . of the Penal Code of China*. London: Cadell and Davies, 1810. Reprint. Taipei: Ch'eng-wen Publishing Co., 1966.

Strawn, Silas H. "The State of China." *Far Eastern Review* 23, no. 1 (Jan. 1927):12–15.

Teichman, Sir Eric. *Affairs of China: A Survey of the Recent History and Present Circumstances of the Republic of China.* London: Methuen, 1938.

Willoughby, Westel W. *Foreign Rights and Interests in China.* 2d rev. edition. Baltimore: Johns Hopkins University Press, 1927.

Wu, John C. H. *Beyond East and West.* New York: Sheed and Ward, 1951. Reprint. Taipei: Mei Ya Publications, 1969.

———. *Fountain of Justice.* Taipei: Mei Ya Publications, 1971.

Yuen, T. T., and Tachuen S. K. Loh, trans. *The Provisional Criminal Code of the Republic of China.* Beijing: Peking Gazette, 1915.

UNPUBLISHED SECONDARY SOURCES

Bell, Randall T. "The Shanghai Mixed Court and the Staple Court of England: An Historical Comparison." Paper submitted to Professor Jerome A. Cohen, Harvard Law School, 1971.

Chang Yun Chao. "Wu Ting-fang's Contribution Towards Political Reforms in the Late Ch'ing period." Ph.D. diss., University of Hong Kong, 1982.

Conner, Alison Wayne. "The Law of Evidence During the Ch'ing Dynasty." Ph.D. diss., Cornell University, 1979.

Du Brock, Roger. "A Study of the Treatment Accorded to Chinese Plaintiffs in the Civil Summary Division of H.B.M.'s Supreme Court for China and Japan from 1875 to 1885 as Evidenced in the Law Reports Contained in the North China Herald." Paper presented to Professor Jerome A. Cohen, Harvard University, 1967.

Park, Bum-Joon Lee. "The British Experience of Counterinsurgency in Malaya: The Emergency 1948–1960." Ph.D. diss., The American University, Washington, D.C., 1965.

Thurston, Richard Lawton. "China's Civil Law Reform Movement, 1912–1930." Ph.D. diss., University of Virginia, 1979.

PUBLISHED SECONDARY SOURCES

Allott, Antony. *The Limits of Law.* London: Butterworths, 1980.

Bao Ruo-wang (Jean Pasqualini) and Rudolf Chelminski. *Prisoner of Mao.* New York: Coward McCann and Geoghegan, 1973.

Bergère, Marie-Claire. "The Other China: Shanghai from 1919 to 1949," in *Shanghai: Revolution and Development in an Asian Metropolis,* ed. Christopher Howe, 1–34. Cambridge: Cambridge University Press, 1981.

Bodde, Derk. *China's First Unifier.* Hong Kong: Hong Kong University Press, 1967.

———, and Clarence Morris. *Law in Imperial China: Exemplified by 190 Ch'ing Dynasty Cases.* Cambridge, Mass.: Harvard University Press, 1967.

Bohannan, Paul. "Ethnography and Comparison in Legal Anthropology," in *Law in Culture and Society*, ed. Laura Nader, 401–18. Chicago: Aldine Press, 1972.

———. *Justice and Judgment among the Tiv*. London: Oxford University Press, 1957.

Bonnichon, André. *Law in Communist China*. The Hague: International Commission of Jurists, n.d. (about 1956).

Boorman, Howard L., and Richard C. Howard. *Biographical Dictionary of Republican China*. New York: Columbia University Press, 1970.

Borg, Dorothy. *American Policy and the Chinese Revolution 1925–1928*. New York: Macmillan, 1947.

Boyle, Francis A. "The Irrelevance of International Law: The Schism between International Law and International Politics." *California Western International Law Journal* 10 (1980):193–219.

Brand, C. E. *Roman Military Law*. Austin: University of Texas Press, 1968.

Brinton, Jasper Yeates. *The Mixed Courts of Egypt*. Rev. ed. New Haven: Yale University Press, 1968.

Bünger, Karl. "Die Rezeption des europaischen Rechts in China." *Deutsche lands-referate zum III. Internationalen Kongres für Rechtsvergleichung in London 1950*, 177–81.

Chang, Chung-li. *The Income of the Chinese Gentry*. Seattle: University of Washington Press, 1962.

Chang, H. C., trans. and ed. *Chinese Literature: Popular Fiction and Drama*. Edinburgh: Edinburgh University Press, 1973.

Chang, Wejen. "The Grand Secretariat Archive and the Study of the Ch'ing Judicial Process." *Ch'ing-shih wen-t'i* 4, no. 5 (June 1981):112–15.

Ch'en, Paul Heng-chao. *Chinese Legal Tradition under the Mongols*. Princeton: Princeton University Press, 1979.

———. "Collective Punishment," in *The Cambridge Encyclopedia of China*, ed. Brian Hook, 123–24. Cambridge: Cambridge University Press, 1982.

Cheng, Bin. *General Principles of Law*. London: Stevens, 1953.

Chesneaux, Jean, and John Lust. *Introduction aux études d'histoire contemporaine de Chine 1898–1949*. Paris: Mouton, 1964.

Ch'ü, T'ung-tsu. *Law and Society in Traditional China*. The Hague: Mouton, 1961. Reprint. Taiwan: Rainbow Bridge, 1965.

———. *Local Government in China under the Ch'ing*. Stanford: Stanford University Press, 1969.

Clarke, R. F., S. J. "The Training of a Jesuit." *The Nineteenth Century* 40 (July–Dec. 1896):211–25.

Clifford, Nicholas R. *Shanghai, 1925: Urban Nationalism and the Defense of Foreign Privilege*. Michigan Papers in Chinese Studies no. 37. Ann Arbor: Center for Chinese Studies, University of Michigan, 1979.

Cohen, Jerome Alan, ed. *China's Practice of International Law: Some Case Studies*. Cambridge, Mass.: Harvard University Press, 1972.

———. "The Chinese Communist Party and Judicial Independence." *Harvard Law Review*, 82, no. 5 (March 1969):967–1007.

———. "Chinese Mediation on the Eve of Modernization," in *Traditional and Modern Legal Institutions in Asia and Africa*, ed. David C. Buxbaum, 54–76. Leiden: E. J. Brill, 1967.

———, ed. *Contemporary Chinese Law: Research Problems and Perspectives*. Cambridge, Mass.: Harvard University Press, 1970.

———. *The Criminal Process in the People's Republic of China, 1949–1963*. Cambridge, Mass.: Harvard University Press, 1968.

———. "Due Process?" in *The China Difference*, ed. Ross Terrill. New York: Harper & Row, 1979.

———, R. Randle Edwards, and Fu-mei Chang Chen, eds. *Essays on China's Legal Tradition*. Princeton: Princeton University Press, 1980.

Cooke, John S. "The U.S. Court of Military Appeals 1975–1977: Judicializing the Military Justice System." *Military Law Review* 76 (1977):43–163.

David, René, and John Brierley. *Major Legal Systems in the World Today*. 2d ed. London: Stevens, 1978.

Derrett, J. Duncan M., ed. *An Introduction to Legal Systems*. London: Sweet & Maxwell, 1968.

———. *Law in the New Testament*. London: Darton Longman & Todd, 1970.

de Smith, S. A. *Judicial Review of Administrative Action*. Ed. J. M. Evans. 4th ed. London: Stevens, 1980.

Dias, R. W. M. *Jurisprudence*. London: Butterworths, 1970.

Drage, Charles. *Taikoo*. London: Constable, 1970.

Dumont, Louis. *Homo Hierarchicus*. Trans. Mark Sainsbury. London: Weidenfeld & Nicolson, 1970.

Eastman, Lloyd E. *The Abortive Revolution: China under Nationalist Rule 1927–1937*. Cambridge, Mass.: Harvard University Press, 1974.

Edwards, R. Randle. "Ch'ing Legal Jurisdiction over Foreigners," in *Essays on China's Legal Tradition*, ed. Jerome A. Cohen et al., 222–69. Princeton: Princeton University Press, 1980.

Elvin, Mark. "The Mixed Court of the International Settlement at Shanghai (Until 1911)," in *Papers on China* 17:131–59. Cambridge, Mass.: East Asian Research Center, Harvard University, 1963.

———. "The Revolution of 1911 in Shanghai," in *Papers on Far Eastern History* 29:119–61. Canberra: Dept. of Far Eastern History, Australian National University, March 1984. 119–61.

———, and G. William Skinner, eds. *The Chinese City between Two Worlds*. Stanford: Stanford University Press, 1974.

Fikentscher, Wolfgang. *Methoden des Rechts in vergleichender Darstellung*. 5 vols. Tubingen: Mohr, 1975–77.

———. "Synepeics in Law and Justice," in *Festschrift fur Constantin Tsatsos*, 557–93. Athens: Juristischer Verlag Ant. N. Sakkoulas, 1980.

Fishel, Wesley R. *The End of Extraterritoriality in China*. Berkeley: University of California Press, 1952.

Forbes, J. R. "University Discipline: A New Province for Natural Justice?" *University of Queensland Law Journal* 7 (1970): 85–108.

Fuller, Lon L. *The Morality of Law*. Rev. ed. New Haven: Yale University Press, 1969.

Fung, Yu-lan. *A Short History of Chinese Philosophy*. Trans. and ed. Derk Bodde. New York: Macmillan, 1948.

Generous, William T., Jr. *Swords and Scales: The Development of the Uniform Code of Military Justice*. Port Washington, N. Y.: Kennikat Press, 1973.

Gilmore, Grant, and Charles L. Black., Jr. *The Law of Admiralty*. 2d ed. New York: Foundation Press, 1975.

Greenhut, Jeffrey. "Sahib and Sepoy: An Enquiry into the Relationship of the British Officers and Native Soldiers of the British Indian Army." *Military Affairs* (U.S.A.) 48, no. 1 (Jan. 1984): 15–18.

Grupp, Stanley E., ed. *Theories of Punishment*. Bloomington: Indiana University Press, 1971.

Hambro, E. "Function of the International Court of Justice in the Framework of the International Legal Order," in *The United Nations: Ten Years of Legal Progress*, ed. Gesina H. J. van der Molen et al. The Hague: Nederlandse Studentenvereniging voor Wereldrechts-orde, 1956.

Hamilton, General Sir Ian. *The Soul and Body of an Army*. London: Arnold, 1921.

Harrison, Judy Feldman. "Wrongful Treatment of Prisoners: A Case Study of Ch'ing Legal Practice." *The Journal of Asiatic Studies* 23, no. 2 (Feb. 1964): 227–44.

Hart, H. L. A. *The Concept of Law*. Oxford: Clarendon Press, 1961.

———. *Punishment and Responsibility*. Oxford: Clarendon Press, 1978.

Hartnett, Major Andrew C.J., U.S.M.C. "Discipline and Justice." *The J.A.G. Journal*, May 1955, 3–7.

Hayden, George A. *Crime and Punishment in Medieval Chinese Drama: Three Judge Pao Plays*. Cambridge, Mass.: Harvard University Press, 1978.

Henderson, Dan Fenno. *Conciliation and Japanese Law: Tokugawa and Modern*. Seattle: University of Washington Press, 1965.

———. "The Evolution of Tokugawa Law," in *Studies in the Institutional History of Early Modern Japan*, ed. John W. Hall and Marius B. Jansen. Princeton: Princeton University Press, 1968.

———. "Japanese Law in English: Reflections on Translation." *Journal of Japanese Studies*, 6, no. 1 (1980): 117–54.

———. "Introduction to the Kujikata Osadamegaki (1742)," in *Hô to keibatsu no rekishi-teki kosatsu* (Historical studies on law and punishment), Editorial Committee for Memorial Essays in Honor of Dr. Hiramatsu Yoshiro, 489–544. Nagoya: Nagoya Daigaku Shuppankai, 1987.

———, and Yoshiro Hiramatsu. *Administration of Justice in Tokugawa Japan: Translation of* Written Provisions Concerning Suits *(Kujikata Osadamegaki) Book I (1742).*

Holdsworth, Sir William. *A History of English Law.* 16 vols. London: Methuen, 1903–66.

Holland, D. C. "The Law of Courts Martial." *Current Legal Problems* 3 (1950): 173–94.

Hooker, M. B. *Legal Pluralism.* Oxford: Clarendon Press, 1975.

Howe, Mark de Wolfe, comp. *The Occasional Speeches of Justice Oliver Wendell Holmes.* Cambridge, Mass.: Belknap Press, 1962.

Hsia, Tao-tai. *Guide to Selected Legal Sources of Mainland China.* Washington: Library of Congress, 1967.

Hsiao, Kung-Chuan. *Rural China: Imperial Control in the Nineteenth Century.* Seattle: University of Washington Press, 1960.

Hsiung, James Chieh. *Law and Policy in China's Foreign Relations.* New York: Columbia University Press, 1972.

Hu Hsien Chin. *The Common Descent Group in China and Its Functions.* New York: Viking Fund, 1948. Reprint. New York: Johnson, 1964.

Hucker, Charles O. *The Censorial System of Ming China.* Stanford: Stanford University Press, 1966.

Hudson, Manley O. "The Rendition of the International Mixed Court at Shanghai." *The American Journal of International Law* 21 (1927): 451–71.

Hulsewé, A. F. P. *Remnants of Han Law.* Leiden: E. J. Brill, 1955.

International Encyclopedia of Comparative Law. Chief ed. René David. 17 vols. The Hague: Mouton, 1975–.

Jardine Matheson & Company: An Historical Sketch. Hong Kong: Jardine Matheson & Company, n.d.

Johnson, Wallace. *The T'ang Code.* Princeton: Princeton University Press, 1979.

Johnston, W. Ross. *Sovereignty and Protection: A Study of British Jurisdictional Imperialism in the Late Nineteenth Century.* Durham, N.C.: Duke University Press, 1973.

Johnstone, William Crane, Jr. *The Shanghai Problem.* Stanford: Stanford University Press, 1937.

Jones, William C. "Studying the Ch'ing Code: The Ta Ch'ing Lu Li." *The American Journal of Comparative Law* 22 (1974): 330–64.

Kamenka, Eugene. "Gemeinschaft and Gesellschaft." *Political Science* (New Zealand) 17, no. 1 (1965): 3–12.

Keeton, George W. "Chinese Law and Historical Jurisprudence." *The Chinese Social and Political Science Review* 12 (1928): 511–15.

———. *The Development of Extraterritoriality in China.* 2 vols. London: Longmans Green, 1928.

Kier, D.L., and F. H. Lawson. *Cases in Constitutional Law.* 5th ed. Oxford: Clarendon Press, 1967.

Krygier, Martin. "Anthropological Approaches," in *Law and Social Control,* ed. Eugene Kamenka and Alice E. Tay, 27–59. London: Edward Arnold, 1980.

Lane-Poole, Stanley. *The Life of Sir Harry Parkes*. 2 vols. London: Macmillan, 1894.

Levenson, Joseph R. *Confucian China and Its Modern Fate*. 3 vols. London: Routledge & Kegan Paul, 1964.

Liu, Shih Shun. *Extraterritoriality: Its Rise and Its Decline*. Studies in History, Economics and Public Law, vol. 118, no. 2, whole number 263. New York: Columbia University, 1925.

McKnight, Brian E. *The Quality of Mercy: Amnesties and Traditional Chinese Justice*. Honolulu: The University Press of Hawaii, 1981.

McLeod, Katrina C. D., and Robin D. S. Yates. "Forms of Ch'in Law: An Annotated Translation of the *Feng-chen shih*." *Harvard Journal of Asiatic Studies* 41, no. 1 (June 1981): 111ff.

Maine, Henry Sumner. *Ancient Law*. London: Oxford University Press, 1931. Reprint 1950. First published 1861.

———. *Dissertation on Early Law and Custom*. London: Murray, 1883.

Mass, Jeffrey P. *The Development of Kamakura Rule 1180–1250*. Stanford: Stanford University Press, 1979.

Maybon, Charles Batiste, and Jean Fredet. *Histoire de la Concession Française de Changhai*. Paris: Librairie Plon, 1929.

Meijer, Marinus J. *The Introduction of Modern Criminal Law in China*. Batavia: De Unie, 1950.

———. *Marriage Law and Policy in the Chinese People's Republic*. Hong Kong: Hong Kong University Press, 1971.

Merson, John. *Culture and Science in China*. Sydney: Australian Broadcasting Commission, 1981.

Michael, Franz. "The Role of Law in Traditional, Nationalist and Communist China." *The China Quarterly* 9 (1962): 124–48.

Mitrano, Thomas. "The Chinese Bankruptcy Law of 1906–1907: A Legislative Case History." *Monumenta Serica* 30 (1972–73): 259–37.

Murphey, Rhoads. *The Outsiders: The Western Experience in India and China*. Ann Arbor: University of Michigan Press, 1977.

Nader, Laura. "The Anthropological Study of Law." *American Anthropologist* 67, no. 6, pt. 2 (Dec. 1965): 3–32.

Nafziger, J. "The Development of International Law: Obstacles and Hopes." *Australian Outlook* 38 (Apr. 1984): 33–39.

Needham, Joseph. *Science and Civilization in China*. 5 vols. Cambridge: Cambridge University Press, 1956–80.

Northrop, F. S. C. *The Meeting of East and West*. New York: Macmillan, 1949.

———. *The Taming of the Nations*. New York: Macmillan, 1952.

———. "Toward a Deductively Formulated and Operationally Verifiable Comparative Cultural Anthropology," in *Cross Cultural Understanding*, ed. F. S. C. Northrop and Helen H. Livingston. New York: Harper & Row, 1964.

Paton, George W., and David P. Derham. *A Textbook of Jurisprudence*. 4th ed. Oxford: Clarendon Press, 1972.

Piggott, Sir Francis. *Extra-territoriality: the Law Relating to Consular Jurisdiction and to Residence in Oriental Countries*. New rev. ed., Hong Kong: Kelly & Walsh, 1907.

Pospisil, Leopold J. *The Ethnology of Law*. 2d ed. Menlo Park, Calif.: Cummings, 1978.

Roberts, Simon. *Order and Dispute: An Introduction to Legal Anthropology*. Harmondsworth: Penguin Books, 1979.

Rowe, Peter J. "Military Justice within the British Army." *Military Law Review* 94 (Fall 1981): 99–134.

Skinner, G. William, ed. *The City in Late Imperial China*. Stanford: Stanford University Press, 1977.

Solomon, Richard H. *Mao's Revolution and the Chinese Political Culture*. Berkeley: University of California Press, 1971.

Sousa, Nasim. *The Capitulatory Regime of Turkey: Its History, Origin and Nature*. Baltimore: Johns Hopkins University Press, 1933.

Spence, Jonathan. *Emperor of China*. London: Jonathan Cape, 1974.

Steadman, John M. *The Myth of Asia*. New York: Simon & Schuster, 1969.

Stephens, Thomas B. "The Ming Sung Umbrella Case." *Australian Journal of Politics and History* 33, no. 2 (1987): 76–89.

———. "The History and Jurisprudence of the Mixed Court of the International Settlement at Shanghai 1911–1927." Ph.D. diss., University of Queensland, 1985.

Stuart-Smith, James. "Military Law: Its History, Administration and Practice." *Law Quarterly Review* 85 (1969): 478–504.

Szaszy, Istvan. *Conflict of Laws in the Western, Socialist and Developing Countries*. Trans. J. Decsenyi. Leiden: A. W. Sijthoff, 1974.

Tay, Alice Ehr-Soon. "Law in Communist China." Part 1. *Sydney Law Review* 6, no. 2 (Oct. 1969): 153–72.

Teiwes, Frederich C. *Elite Discipline in China*. Canberra: Contemporary China Centre, Australian National University Press, 1978.

Tonnies, Ferdinand. *Community and Society*. Trans. and ed. Charles P. Loomis. New York: Harper & Row, 1957.

Ullmann, Walter. *Principles of Government and Politics in the Middle Ages*. London: Methuen, 1961. Reprint 1977.

van Gulik, R. H. *Tang-yin-pi-shih "Parallel Cases from under the Pear Tree": A Thirteenth Century Manual of Jurisprudence and Detection*. Trans. R. H. van Gulik. Leiden: E. J. Brill, 1956.

van der Valk, Marc. *An Outline of Modern Chinese Family Law*. Beijing: Henri Vetch, 1939.

———. "Custom in Modern Chinese Private Law." *Monumenta Serica* 30 (1972–73): 220–58.

———, trans. and ed. *Interpretations of the Supreme Court at Peking—Years 1915 and 1916*. Batavia: Sinological Institute, University of Indonesia, 1949.

Wade, E. C. S. "Act of State in English Law: Its Relation with International Law." *The British Year Book of International Law* 15 (1934): 98–112.

Wade, H. W. R. *Administrative Law*. 5th ed. Oxford: Clarendon Press, 1982.

Waley, Arthur. *Three Ways of Thought in Ancient China*. London: Geo. Allen & Unwin, 1939.

Walton, Clifford. *History of the British Standing Army A.D. 1660 to 1700*. London: Harrison & Sons, 1894.

Watson, G. R. *The Roman Soldier*. London: Thames and Hudson, 1981.

Watt, John R. *The District Magistrate in Late Imperial China*. New York: Columbia University Press, 1972.

Weber, Max. *Economy and Society: An Outline of Interpretive Sociology*. Ed. Guenther Roth and Claus Wittich, trans. Max Rheinstein et al. 3 vols. New York: Bedminster Press, 1968.

Wei Min. "Reforming Criminals." *Beijing Review* no. 8 (23 Feb. 1981): 22–29.

Wiener, Frederick B. "Advocacy at Military Law: the Lawyers's Reason and the Soldier's Faith." *Military Law Review* 80 (1978): 1–28.

Wigmore, John Henry. *Law and Justice in Tokugawa Japan*. 10 parts. Tokyo: Kokusai Bunka Shinkokai, 1969–76.

———. *A Panorama of the World's Legal Systems*. St. Paul: West Publishing Co., 1928. Reprint. Washington: Washington Law Book Co., 1936.

———. "Some Lessons for Civil Justice to Be Learned from Federal Military Justice." *Maryland State Bar Association Transactions* 24 (1919): 188.

Williams, Glanville. *Textbook of Criminal Law*. London: Stevens, 1978.

Wittfogel, Karl A. *Oriental Despotism*. New Haven: Yale University Press, 1957.

Woodcock, George. *The British in the Far East*. London: Wiedenfeld & Nicolson, 1969.

Wu Ching-tzu. *The Scholars*. Beijing: Foreign Languages Press, 1957.

Zhou Zeng, and Liu Bin. "Bid Farewell to Yesterday: A Reformatory near Qinhuangdao." *Beijing Review* no. 3 (17 Jan. 1983): 19–25.

Zilsel, E. "The Genesis of the Concept of Physical Law." *The Philosophical Review* 51 (1942) 245–79.

Index

Thomas Blacket Stephens served as a solicitor and attorney of the Supreme Court of Queensland, Australia, from 1926 to 1966. During World War II he was posted to the Australian Army Legal Department, saw active service abroad, and became Chief Legal Officer at Headquarters Second Australian Corps. In 1970 he returned to full-time academic studies, and he received his doctorate from the University of Queensland in 1985.

www.ingramcontent.com/pod-product-compliance
Lightning Source LLC
LaVergne TN
LVHW050227080826
844660LV00012B/488

* 9 7 8 0 2 9 5 9 7 1 2 3 0 *